Who Turned On the Lights in Attalla?

By

Editor Martha Lou Riddle

To Caroline and Hal
Enjoy
Martha Lou
Feb. 05

authorHOUSE™

1663 LIBERTY DRIVE, SUITE 200
BLOOMINGTON, INDIANA 47403
(800) 839-8640
WWW.AUTHORHOUSE.COM

First published by AuthorHouse 10/20/04

ISBN: 1-4184-8807-0 (sc)
ISBN: 1-4184-8806-2 (dj)

Printed in the United States of America
Bloomington, Indiana

This book is printed on acid-free paper.

Table of Contents

History of Attalla, Alabama

Prepared by George P. Walker, III

Listed on the Internet under History of Attalla, Alabama

In the beginning "God Herself" probably smiled on Attalla. Judge for yourself as you read the research prepared by George P. Walker, III in 1955. He has graciously consented to allow "Who Turned on the Lights in Attalla?" to use his research which is well documented.

"Attalla's history actually predates its incorporation as a town. LaFayette visited what is now Attalla in 1825, as a guest of the U. S. Government. A French writer, Courter B. Chateaubriand, was also a visitor and wrote a novel on "Atala, an Indian maiden." *1

The town occupies the site of an Indian village which was of considerable importance during the Creek War. It was the home of Captain John Brown, a famous Indian, whose daughters, Catharine and Anna, established the Creek Path Mission school in 1820, six miles south of Guntersville. It was in Attalla that David Brown, an Indian, assisted by the Rev. D. S. Butterick, prepared the "Cherokee Spelling Book."

1

Early settlers to this area were W. C. Hammond, Henry W. Pickens, Dr. Thomas Edwards, Rev. James Scales, John Latham, E. I. Holcomb, John S. Moragne, and Allen Gray, who became the first postmaster.

Indian relics of the vicinity are "Tsu-sanya-sah –Ruins-of-a-Great-City," and site of the home of Captain John Brown. *2

Attalla was incorporated as a city government on February 5, 1872, after being founded in 1870 on land donated for the site of the town by W. C. Hammond, a plantation owner. An early business enterprise was a bowling alley in a pine thicket. *3

Attalla's population has remained diminutive in number, but with that small quantity, it has shown dramatic growth throughout the town's incorporated life. This is illustrated by the following year, population numbers. 1872-300; 1888-400; 1916-4,000; 1940-4,585; 1952-7,537. *4

The name "New Town" was likely changed to "Newton" between 1832 and 1840. Newton was the name Attalla used until February 21, 1870, when "Attalla" was selected as the name for the post office location.

The town was officially named "Attalla" in 1893. *5

E. I. Holcomb served as the first Mayor of Attalla.

There are several opinions as to how the town got the name "Attalla" and what this name actually means. In a rare book on place-names in Alabama, the author states: "Attalla - a city in Etowah County. The first settlement here was called Atale, which is a corruption of the Cherokee word "otali", or "mountain." *6

"My Home" is the most generally accepted meaning for the name Attalla. Ed Hamner was one of the most erudite men of Attalla in Indian affairs and lore. He served as chairman of the local board of education in Attalla. Regarded as an authority on both ancient and modern history, he was known throughout the area as the leading authority on the Cherokee, Choctaw, and Creek Indians. He also had a small library of rare and expensive books. His claim that Attalla means "My Home" is accepted by most authorities today. *7

In 1870, Stanton, Cravath, and Stanton, promoters of West Newton, Massachusetts, had completed their Wills Valley railroad from Chattanooga, TN, along the base of historic Lookout Mountain to its southern extremity, where Attalla is now located. There they halted operations long enough to build a large hotel and to lay out a town, which they called Newton, in honor of their old hometown in Massachusetts. It was there also that the newly chartered road, the Selma, Rome, and Dalton Railroad, came into existence, through the enterprise of the citizens of Gadsden and Guntersville. Thus the railroad crossing became a reality, and a part of the Nashville & Chattanooga Railroad system. Later still, the Alabama Mineral Railroad was merged into the Louisville & Nashville system, and this made Attalla the converging center of these great railroads. The Wills Valley Railroad had become the Alabama Great Southern, and part and parcel of the Southern Railway System.

When "Newton," the town promoted by Stanton, Cravath, and Stanton, grew to sufficient proportions, a post office was requested. There being already a "Newton" post office in the state, they were forced to select another name, and "Attalla" was selected. The name is supposed to have been selected by early French settlers from the name of the heroine, "Atala," in a popular novel at the time. It should not be over-looked, however, that many Cherokee Indians had lived in this section, and that the Cherokees were divided into two classes. Those at home or near their head town were called, Atali," and those away from home, sometimes classed as hunters, were called "Erati" Cherokees. Thus it will be seen that the word from which the present name, "Attalla," was derived, is a Cherokee word applied to Indians at home, and is generally accepted as meaning "home" and "my home."

Miss Ida Hamner believes that the Indian village that used to be where Attalla is now, was called "Otali," meaning "mountain," after which Attalla may have been named. Otali was one of the chief Indian villages of the Cherokee nation. Her brother, Ed Hamner, has made note of certain places in the present corporate limits of the town where Indian families definitely lived.

George Guest (Se-Quo-Yah), son of Colonel Nathaniel Guest and his Indian wife, who was a sister of the celebrated "Peace Chief" Ke-ahat-a-he, as a boy migrated with his mother (the father being listed as one of the casualties of the battle of King's Mountain in the American Revolution), and settled in Big Wills Valley. But he was no doubt a familiar figure in all of the Cherokee towns in the Valley, as he was a blacksmith, silversmith, and an all-round mechanic before he invented his Cherokee alphabet, and made tomahawks and such other things as his people of the Valley used or needed. He was recognized as the greatest of his race in this part of the country. Congress voted him a largess of $500, and had his picture painted and placed in the government archives at Washington, D.C., voted $1,000 to his people with which to buy a printing press, and "Cherokee alphabet" type; and $20,000 for the establishment and maintenance of Indian schools, while the Cherokees themselves, through their council, voted Sequoyah a medal. This occurred shortly after Sequoyah voluntarily migrated to the west, in about 1823. *8

One of the most distinguished men in Attalla's history was Commodore Ebenezar Farrand. He served in both the United

States Navy and the Confederate States Navy. When the Civil War began, Farrand, a staunch believer and supporter of the Confederate cause, left his home, friends, and family and joined the Confederate Navy. When the war ended, he became an insurance representative in Montgomery, Alabama. In 1879, when the Alabama Great Southern Railroad was built through Attalla, and a hotel was built on the railroad property there to serve as a depot and as an eating place, he went to Attalla and became the first one to operate it. This hotel, a replica of the famous Stanton House in Chattanooga, was one of the town's most outstanding landmarks until it was either burned or dismantled in the 1950's. When he died in 1873, Farrand was buried in the old Attalla cemetery, which was later abandoned. Mrs. M. E. McKenzie, a friend who knew him as a great gentleman, placed a stone marker at his grave. Later her adopted daughter, the late Mrs. Lalla Rock Forman, organized the Farrand Chapter of the Daughters of the Confederacy and selected as one of its first projects the placing of an appropriate marker in downtown Attalla (placed at the "Y" where 3rd and 4th Streets merge.) It was later removed as a traffic hazard and was placed on the Attalla City School grounds in June of 1947.

Judge Henry W. Pickens made the first move to establish a school and a church here in 1872, when he purchased the sites and donated them to the town with the condition that the property be used for no other purpose. He was an early postmaster of Attalla, and an officer in the Confederate Army. His grave in the old Attalla cemetery remains as one of the few marked graves. *9

In 1889, C. D. Henley, who later became the first mayor of Birmingham, built a brick building. Henley's building became the bank of Attalla on July 12, 1889, the first bank recognized as such in Attalla and the second in Etowah County. In 1906, its name was changed to the First National Bank. *10

The first church in Attalla, a Presbyterian church, was built in 1851, when the surrounding area was farmland and woodlands. The second church, Northern Methodist (Methodist Episcopal), was built in 1860, before Attalla was surveyed. The first school was held in that church, and the people sat on half logs with pegs for legs. A Southern Methodist Episcopal church was erected in 1865. In 1887, a Baptist church was organized in the Clements school house by Hamilton Ralls of Gadsden, Mrs. L. E. Harrison, and Mrs. W. S. White. After Attalla incorporated, there were two schools; the Hudson School and the Clements School. The Hudson school was the first and was taught by the Reverend M. Clements. Besides teaching at his school, Reverend Clements preached at the Methodist church. The two schools had a keen rivalry between them, and "school butter" was the forsaken word, such as "bell hop" is for certain military schools today to arouse a fighting school spirit. In 1891, the two schools were consolidated across town in the first brick building constructed for a school. This school was taught by E. O. McCord. *11

During reconstruction, P. J. Smith was sent south by a northern concern to set up Republican newspapers in towns and cities of the South. He called his newspaper the "Republican Union" and began publication in Attalla on Friday, May 20, 1870. This was the first newspaper ever published in Attalla. It was radical in politics and thus did not survive long. Smith also operated the Attalla Hotel for a short period after the death of Commodore Farrand. *12

"In 1885, the "Pick and Shovel" newspaper was established - the name being the embodiment of industry - probably due to the fact that Attalla had become the largest iron ore shipping point in Alabama. When the "Pick and Shovel" gave up the struggle, the "Crescent" became its successor." *13. Next came the "New Age," then the Attalla "Herald," published by G. Thomas Moore, and later J. W. Mills, Attalla's only newspaper in 1955 was "The Etowah News Journal."

Attalla was prosperous until the railroads, upon which it depended, went into bankruptcy. After that, the town had a precarious existence for almost a decade. The subsequent resuscitation of the railroads did not benefit Attalla, at least for some time, because trade went to other places and through other channels; also some of its most prominent businessmen relocated elsewhere, thus depriving it of a very important auxiliary to progress. The town remained in a stagnant, listless condition until the opening of the iron mines in the surrounding mountains. The development of this new industry, with all its various accompaniments, put life and vigor into the area and started it on a safe and solid road to prosperity.

John S. Moragne bought mineral lands at Attalla in 1859, and sank what was probably the first iron ore shaft in Northeast Alabama. In 1871, he shipped the first carload of iron ore by rail out of the state, to Wheeling, West Virginia. *14 He was perhaps the first person to call attention to the rich coal and iron deposits in North Alabama. "In the 1880's his collection of minerals, gathered during his wanderings over this part of the state, won the first prize at the state fair. He and John W. Duncan, his son-in-law, hauled the ore from the first Attalla mine to the railroad in wagons Their mining methods were rather primitive as compared to modern methods. The Moragne estate owned much more land near Attalla. One large section was sold in the 1890's to a Chattanooga concern for $45,000, but it did not include the operating mines later owned by the Sloss-Sheffield Mining Company.

"In the late 1880's, Attalla was noted as being the largest iron ore shipping point in the state. At first the ore was hauled from the mines by horse drawn wagon and piled at the corner of Fifth Avenue and the Alabama Great Southern Railroad. It was probably loaded on the train by men wielding shovels, then shipped to furnaces in Chattanooga and Birmingham, and finally taken to Gadsden furnaces." *15

After the wagons became impractical, small dummy trains were used to haul the ore from the mines. Ben Stewart was a conductor on one of these small trains for years. He and Obal Christopher made up the first of Christopher & Stewart which ran the commissary to their mine and cotton gin. Stewart was Mayor of Attalla at one time. The Christopher and Stewart store was the first of its kind in Attalla, and was one of the main stores in town. *16

Before Attalla was incorporated, it was called the "Junction." In 1893, an article appeared in the Attalla "Herald" which said, "Attalla is a city made by the railroads. It grew because it had to grow, and the railroads came because they had to, and will have to come, to get away from the mountains. Its destiny is fixed by its location, and its people are alive to this fact, and the active bustling town is a living example of present prosperity." *17

The East Alabama & Cincinnati Railroad was constructed through Attalla and went on as far as Gadsden. This was Attalla's first railroad to Gadsden. Later the T. & C. Railroad went through, and in 1890, the Gadsden-Attalla Dummy Line did also. The first railroad to Birmingham, the L. & N. Railroad, was first built to Attalla and then stopped for awhile. Its first run through to Birmingham was made on May 23, 1905. That first train had its last run on January 30, 1951.

The first electric generator operated by water was built in September 1882, at Appleton, Wisconsin. The first hydro-electric plant for lighting a whole town was invented on a stream in Etowah County near Attalla by W. P. Lay in 1887. This invention in Attalla led to the creation of the Southern Company and Alabama Power.

In that same year, Attalla had its first big fire. It was on the northeast side of Fifth Avenue between Third and Fourth

Streets. All the buildings were made of wood, but luckily the fire only burned in one direction. The second big fire, the most disastrous in the history of Attalla, occurred in 1891. Between the times of these fires, brick buildings were being erected throughout the area, affected by the first fire. These were the first brick buildings to be constructed in Attalla. The second fire burned in both directions, and swept through all buildings between Third and Fourth Streets, demolishing all except three small wooden shanties. It was difficult to bring the blaze under control, because the town had no waterworks and had to depend upon a bucket brigade. *18

First Baptist Church of Attalla was organized in 1887 under the pastorate of Rev. Henry Edward Harris. He was actually successor to Rev. Hamilton Blount Ralls who was a Baptist Missionary sent to Attalla in 1885, but Rev. Ralls only held meetings in the old Clements School. Rev. Harris was responsible for organizing the church. The stone-constructed sanctuary and buildings were the second major facility occupied by the First Baptist Church. The property was obtained on March 17, 1925 and the cornerstone laid on June 7, 1925 as construction began. The first service was held in it on Wednesday, November 11, 1925. The building was demolished in 1980 to make room for a more modern addition to the present main sanctuary which had been built behind this structure in 1960.

In June, 1891, Attalla awarded a contract to Hartford, Herbert and Company of Chattanooga to build a water works within its limits, and ordered work to begin within 30 days. With this step, Attalla began its career of municipal ownership, and in due time, the city built its own electric and telephone systems. Except for the financial panic that soon started, the venture would have been a success. The telephone and electric systems were sold first, and then the water plant was disposed of to a private concern. One of the conditions of the sale of the water plant was that the new owners would not raise water rates. Within 30 days after the transaction, the company asked the state public utilities commission for permission to advance rates higher. The Supreme Court ruled in favor of the water company. Years later, the City of Attalla purchased the water distribution system, which was all that was left of the original system. It continued the policy of the private concern to purchase water from the Gadsden water plant. *19

In 1890, the question arose whether to put the county courthouse in Attalla or in Gadsden. A committee of five people convened to discuss and vote on the matter. Commissioners J. B. Washburn and E. A. Gilliland voted to move the county courthouse site to Attalla. Commissioners John W. Miller and Dan G. McCuley voted to retain it in Gadsden. Probate Judge James A. Tallman, the official chairman, broke the tie by voting for Gadsden. It has been said that if Attalla had gotten the courthouse in that vote, the situation of Gadsden's much greater population growth and Attalla's growth would have been reversed.

In 1914, a serious effort to consolidate Alabama City and Attalla failed, because the mayor and aldermen of Alabama City balked at the idea at the last moment. J. W. Mills, the clever editor and publisher of the Attalla "Herald" said the plan misfired because of interference by certain Gadsden Citizens. The Gadsden papers, however claimed that the city, as a whole, was not interested. "One alderman was the cause of all the trouble, "Mills wrote, "because of misrepresentation by Gadsden people who are telling the Alabama City people that Attalla wants to gobble them up for selfish gain." He said that Captain J. M. Elliot, Jr. was reported to have told the people of Alabama City that he had no objections to Alabama City "swallowing" Attalla, but he did object to Attalla "swallowing" Alabama City. It seems strange, said the "Herald," "That he (Captain Elliott) should be so all-fired interested when he doesn't live in either town." "The Herald" said the officials of the Dwight Manufacturing Company, a large cotton mill which largely made up Alabama City, had favored the merger.

The truth was that Captain Elliott founded Alabama City in 1891, and he always wanted the three towns to unite under that name. He wanted to create an industrial center in the area, and did a great deal toward realizing that ambition. Alabama City was his "child" and he never deviated from his campaign for it to absorb both Attalla and Gadsden. In 1931, Alabama City voted by a large majority to merge with Gadsden. *21

Camp Siebert, primarily in Attalla, was situated in Etowah and St. Clair Counties, Alabama, as a replacement training center for the Chemical Warfare Service by the Department of Defense between 1942 and 1944. The 37,034 acre site was used as a chemical warfare service training center until April 1945. Training included such tasks as smoke screening, chemical decontamination, chemical depot maintenance and chemical impregnation work. During training exercises, fuming sulfuric acid, or FS was dropped on troops from airplanes to simulate an aerial mustard attack. After decontamination, the land was transferred back to private ownership in 1948. The airfield, however, was transferred to the City of Gadsden.

Will I. Martin once said: "Today there is not a more progressive town in Alabama than Attalla. It is a community of fine homes, wonderful people, and a very great promise for the future. It has good government, excellent schools, and enterprising business men. Many of its boosters in the early days lived to prove that they were not far wrong in 1870." *22

In the fall of 1902, Captain William Patrick Lay, of Gadsden, began construction of a small hydro electric generating plant at the site of Wesson Mill on Big Wills Creek, just southwest of Attalla. The plant was constructed, In Lay's words, "First to supply the City of Attalla with electricity; second, to pump water into a tall stand pipe which would furnish Attalla with water, and third, to demonstrate the possibilities and economy of hydro electric power for which I had been contending for a number of years preceding. When the plant was completed, a line was strung from the 75-horsepower turbine driven generator, over the mountain to a light on a pole in the heart of Attalla. Captain Lay himself threw the switch, bringing electricity to the Community.

Four years later on, December 4th, 1906 Captain Lay organized the Alabama Power Company. Drawing on the success of his experiment at Big Wills Creek, Captain Lay focused his attention on an ambitious plan to develop a high dam and power plant at Lock 12 on the Coosa River. Lock 12 dam, now called Lay Dam, was the first large scale hydro plant built by Alabama Power Company and along with subsequent hydro and steam generating plants, became the foundation on which the Southern Company system of integrated power companies is based today.

When Alabama Power Company reorganized in 1912 and acquired the Attalla system, it discovered that in order to enlist the support of Attalla in the Big Wills Creek project, Captain Lay had agreed to provide the city with free electricity for lighting. That agreement transferred to Alabama Power Company and to this day, schools and other city buildings have two meters - one for free lights and another for billed service.

Did you know that Attalla was the first US city to have electric street lights and was also the birthplace of Alabama Power Company?

This history was edited and somewhat updated for the Internet Portal of the City of Attalla, Alabama, on 2/16,2002 and most content herein was taken from an undated article, "History of Attalla," by George P. Walker III, likely written between 1955-1958   Thank you, George P. Walker III (He made an A on his term paper.)

*1 Jack House, Excerpts from "The Birmingham News, Jan. 8, 1947

*2 Thomas M. Owen, History of Alabama, S. J. Clarke Publishing Co. 1921,1952

*3 Will I. Martin, Gadsden Times, April 29, 1952

*4 Owen, op.cit., 72

*5 Miss Ida Hamner, Interview at Attalla, March 21, 1954

*6 William A. Reed, Indian Place-Names in Alabama

*7 Martin, Gadsden Times, August 27, 1948

*8 Hamner, Gadsden Times, 1929

*9 Miss Ida Hamner, Interview at Attalla, March 23, 1954, and Martin, Gadsden Times.

*10 Miss Ida Hamner, interview March 23, 1954

*11 Miss Hamner, Interview, March 23, 1954

*12 Mrs. R. P. Gant, Interview March 19, 1954

*13 Martin, Gadsden Times, April 29, 1952

*14 Unlisted

*15 Martin, Gadsden Times, January 23, 1953

*16 Miss Hamner, interview March 14, 1954

*17 June 9, 1893 The Hill Country of Alabama, U.S.A. or the Land of Rest, London and New York

*18 Miss Hamner, interview, March 23, 1954 and Martin, "If Memory Serves," compiled by Frances Underwood from articles in the Gadsden Times

*19 Martin, Gadsden Times, "If Memory Serves"

*20 Partially from Martin, Gadsden Times, August 11, 1947

*21 Martin, Gadsden Times, "If Memory Serves"

Memories of Attalla

- Contributed by Ruth Terrell Bailey

E.I. (Bert) Holcomb was the first mayor of Attalla. He used to run a Saloon-Grocery in one of the oldest buildings in Attalla on Fourth Street. It was demolished a few years ago. The last business there was Dewey Rowan's Bargain Barn. When the men would come in on pay day to buy their alcohol, Holcomb's wife would give free groceries out the back door to the wives.

At one time Holcomb owned all the land from Third Street beginning at the entrance to town, all the way up to the main part of town; but because he fell on hard times, he could not pay the taxes and lost possession of it. The land was not developed for years except for Dream Land Lake, located between Third and Fourth Streets, that was used for swimming. People could not get a clear title until the statute of limitation had run out.

Holcomb's wife passed away early and he was left with 5 small girls to rear. Clara Josephine was the oldest and was my grandmother. We used to play under a sycamore tree near a spring across from Johnson's Giant Foods. The other girls were Fannie, Nellie, Sudie, and ?. Clara married a Parrott, then Henry Terrell. Fannie and Nellie married Stanfields.

Many of the descendants live in this part of Alabama now. The Melton Terrells of the Flea Market are some, just to name one family. Sudie married a Henderson.

Attalla was established in 1870 and incorporated as a city government on February 5, 1872. It now boasts of 3 blocks of Antique Shops, affordable housing, a great school system, a progressive service and growth-oriented city government, just to name a few things—according to an ad in The Gadsden Times, Nov. 2, 2003.

Memories of Attalla through Mary Ellen Stewart whose grandmother was Lalla B. Forman

After the War Between the States my great great uncle, P.J. Smith, and his wife, Mary Ellen Barnett, came to north Alabama. Though he was called P.J., his name was John Paul. A newspaper man in Virginia and a Confederate spy during the war. He was offered a job opening newspapers in the South. He felt that he had fought the good fight, it was over, and that the country had to move on toward recovery. So he started "The Republican Union" papers in several places, including Lebanon (then the county seat of DeKalb) and Centre, before coming to Gadsden where he opened the paper and operated The Kittrell House. The business cards for the hotel stated that "The Kittrell House was the "only second-class hotel in the world" and owned by P.J. Smith "the meanest man in America." In earlier years of my life I have read copies of "The Republican Union" from Lebanon, Centre, Gadsden and Attalla, and I don't recall being struck by a radical best as has been stated in recent writings. P. J. was a great wit, and I doubt that he took politics seriously. Prominent items in the paper were legal ads, poetry, interesting stories from all over and upbeat editorials. A large number of the ads for goods and services were from Chattanooga, and for many years I think, it was the main city for major shopping in this area.

With the May 20, 1870 edition the paper moved to Attalla. According to the editorial this was the place to be - "the lucidity of Attalla's facilities has totally obscured that of its satelites - of its neighboring towns." Within six months the site which had been about 100 acres of cotton and a lone log cabin had become "a thriving village composed of over 100 inhabitants; 4 dry goods establishments, 3 family groceries, 2 or 3 (they say) retail groceries; a large and commodious Hotel nearly completed; a printing office, buildings going up as if by magic, streets graded; a Railroad; steam engines heralding the advancement of civilization and internal improvement." With a vision "of fertile valleys surrounded by mountains of great mineral wealth and a convergence of railroads," Uncle P.J. saw a future Attalla with 100's of buildings and 1,000's of businesses on a par with the very largest cities in Alabama. He and Aunt Ellen felt so strongly about this that they invested in property here rather than Birmingham - excellent choice. The slight poem "Attalla-My Home" first appeared anonymously in this issue of the paper. I have often wondered if Uncle P.J. whipped this up in a fit of enthusiasm for the new town.

Commodore Ebenezer Farrand (Capt. Farrand of the U.S. Navy) brought his ship south to join the Confederate cause and took part in several naval battles including Mobile Bay. He surrendered the last ships of the Confederacy to the United States. He stayed in Alabama, first in Montgomery in the insurance business, and in 1871 he came to Attalla to run the hotel ("Railroad House"). Though he had a family in Connecticut and corresponded, he never returned to the north. He became a close friend of Uncle P.J. and Aunt Ellen who remembered him always as an outstanding gentleman and caring companion. She was with him when he died and handled his affairs afterward. Contacting his family she was told to bury him and sell his belongings, settle his accounts and send any remaining money. He was buried in the old cemetery in Attalla and Uncle P.J. had a Wilson in Happy Hollow cut a gravestone.

Aunt Ellen often spoke of the large cemetery that existed in 1870 located in the area past the old Baptist Church on 4th Street. She said it held Indians, blacks, whites, the works. My mother said she always noticed a child's footstone near the gate of the Victorian house where her great aunt Liza Moore lived.

My grandmother, Lalla Rookkh Blankenship, was brought to Attalla in 1884 by Aunt Ellen to spend the winter. She was a frail 9 year old, and it was believed she would not survive another winter in Virginia. She stayed on and, shortly afterward her parents and other relatives came down to Attalla. In 1886 P.J. and Ellen lost their only child, Nancy, age 20, who had a heart attack in Atlanta during the Charleston earthquake, and two years later P.J. died at home. Both were buried under the magnolia tree in the yard of their house. They were moved to Oak Hill Cemetery after the death of Aunt Ellen in 1924. This situation enhanced the belief among some locals that the house was haunted. In the late 1890's Aunt Ellen married a widower from south Alabama, Peter R. McKenzie, who predeceased her by many years.

My grandmother, Lalla B Forman, had many happy memories of Attalla and Gadsden in the 80's and 90's. A favorite pastime for young ladies and their gentleman callers was to walk to the depot and "watch them make a run." She said "it lit up the sky." They would gather at Elliot's Park where there was a lake and boats, a ridge and an open air pavilion. She loved to talk about the wonderful dances under the falls and at the Bellevue Hotel. A very active theatre group of which she was a member put on productions complete with scenery and elegant costumes. Invitations to "at home" gatherings were written out and hand delivered by small boys who made pocket change.

In 1896 my great grandparents, Robert Henry and Emeline Bray Forman, came to Alabama from the North via Somerset, Ky. They leased and operated depot hotels built by the railroad, and he was also in banking. He had been a colonel in the Union Army and was always called "Col." Even by his son. According to the family he was a much-loved, entertaining and good-natured addition to the growing community. Emeline gave the first $100 for the building of the new Methodist Church. Their son, Dr. Charles Bray Forman, graduated from the University of Cincinnati Medical School in 1896 and came down for a visit. He stayed. I lately ran across an invitation which read: "The Young Men of Attalla invite you to Their Seventh Annual Ball at the Forman Hotel, Tuesday evening, Dec. 27th, at nine o'clock, 1898" and stationery headed "The Commercial Club of Attalla, Alabama, Coal, Iron, Manufacturing and Railroad Centre; Pres.: Charles B. Forman; Vice-Pres.: Ed D. Hamner and D. A. Hughes" - more visions of a turn-of-the century mini-metropolis.

I always enjoyed the story about Mr. Underwood, a federal agent who came into town on the train and rented a horse for the following day. He rode off toward Chandler Mt. to track down and arrest the folks making illegal whiskey. At sundown the horse returned without Underwood. It was many years later that one who lived up there told Aunt Ellen that they had plowed all night to obscure evidence of a fresh grave.

The "campground" intrigued me. I don't know exactly where it was, but apparently it was a gathering place (perhaps on Sunday afternoons) with some coming in wagons and on horseback to discuss the latest news, electioneer and gossip. I have a fading picture of Lalla Forman standing in the back of a wagon making a political speech.

Uncle Jim Moore was robbed, shot and died on the steps of the Methodist Church at supper-time one summer. He had arrived on the train from New Orleans and was on his way home. It was assumed that the gunman had been on the train and followed him. No one was arrested though a witness saw the man fleeing and gave a good description. My grandmother said they were never able to remove the blood stains from the steps of the church, and I remember as a child looking at the purported stains many times.

My grandparents were greatly entertained by Elbert Hubbard and his writings. When Hubbard wrote a witty article about the train depot in East Aurora, N.Y. being the dirtiest depot in the U.S., he invited his readers to submit essays on their depots. Lalla gleefully entered the contest with a piece on the Attalla depot. She won first prize. Great sadness attended the household when Hubbard and his wife went down on the Lusitania.

At Etowah High School in 1910 three scholarships worth $100 each were given by C. B. Forman, T.C. Banks, and the Attalla Industrial Club. This covered boarding ($10 monthly) and fees for a year. Lodgings for girls were on the second floor, boys were put up at other locations, and dining was in the basement.

Lalla founded the Forrest Chapter of the U.D.C. in 1916. It was later renamed the Farrand Chapter when the group placed a memorial to Farrand at First St. and Fifth Ave. It is now located at the merging of U.S. Hwy 11 and 4th street. The Attalla Study Club was formed in 1916 with impressive programs on English literature, great historical figures and so on.

Lula Vollmer, playright and screen writer, was born and spent part of her youth in Attalla. She attained worldwide recognition with "Sun-Up", a play about Southern mountain folks which enjoyed many revivals and was even the basis for an opera. Among her many other works she wrote the screenplay for "Spitfire" in 1934 starring Katherine Hepburn. She died in N.Y. in 1955 and is buried in Oak Hill with her parents.

My childhood memories of Attalla are happy ones centered in an enthusiastic and hard-working household where we sat down to three meals each day (chicken and ice cream on Sunday) and participated in good conversations about current news and the important things in life. My grandfather didn't allow back-benchers. As written in his obituary he was a charitable man instrumental in getting industry to Attalla and helping provide good public education. Though he had other interests Attalla always came first. The same could be said about my grandmother. I heard somewhere that the Attalla bank was one of only two in the state during the depression that never closed its doors and paid every depositor who wanted his money. I have never verified that. Isn't it interesting that none of us had any money and were just hoping to "get by," and yet I think there was a genuine optimism about the future and a concern to treat people with kindness.

Forty or so years ago I realized there was a void in my life that I couldn't put my finger on. After some time it suddenly struck me that I was missing the strangers who ate supper at our house almost every night. It was always a lone man and generally, a fascinating one. Our house was marked. Not two blocks from the railroad this was a place to get something to eat. You would not be turned away.

From a Journal of Trip to Mexico

written by May Templin Cole

1936

May Templin Cole was the daughter of Mr. and Mrs. Maurice Templin who came from Tennessee to Attalla. Mr. Templin was a contractor for the building of the Methodist Episcopal Church South (now The First United Methodist Church) in 1903. This church, designated a National Historical Building is still actively in use at the corner of Fourth Street and Sixth Avenue, celebrating its 100th Anniversary on May 2, 2004. The following is from the Journal of Mrs. Cole from her daughter, Katherine Templin Cole Frame, written in the summer of 1936 regarding a trip to Mexico and the opening of the Pan American Highway. The four women were Mae Brown Jones, Kate Wise Brown, May Templin Cole, all of Attalla, and Dorothy Howell Nichols of Gadsden. Unfortunately the first few pages are missing so Mrs. Cole's journal begins:

".....June 30 finds us in Laredo; we had hoped to get in the city in time to see an AAA official and get our necessary papers filled out so as to get an early start next morning but we were too late. He had already left his office—so we got located for the night, had supper under the moon in some pretty garden, then decided to look up a man whom Mae's

Uncle in Jacksonville, Texas had referred us to as a friend of his who had spent a goodly part of his life in Mexico and who would no doubt be able to give us some valuable advice. We found him with very little trouble, spending the evening at home with his daughter. They were indeed charming people and we felt that the time we spent with them was truly profitable. He assured us that we would be quite safe, that the Mexican government was making every possible effort to secure the safety of tourists etc., so I wrote my Mother a card from there telling her of my plans to go in Mexico, she had thrown up her hands in horror and predicted for sure that the bandits would get us while my husband patted me on the back and said in a confident voice that Mae Jones and I would out trick all the bandits in Mexico. So July 1 finds us up early making necessary arrangements to cross the Rio grande into old Mexico. But to our dismay we find that this day is the official opening of the Pan American Highway and many celebrities from various corners of the USA are there including Vice-President Garner, so the bridge is closed, consequently we are delayed several hours. Nevertheless, regardless the terrific heat, we attempt to get near the celebration, rubbing elbows with all colors and hues. In the meantime we are attracted to two nice looking women who are quite outstanding in a crowd like this. They pass by us several times looking impatient. They evidently are anxious to get across the border too. However 'tis around 11:00 o'clock when the bridge is finally thrown open to traffic. On account of excess traffic we lost another hour, with inspections and general routine. When I start to pay for bonding the car and my passport, I find I do not have the exact amount of money and the officials do not seem to have correct change, however they do not speak English, and I am having my very first experience with Mexican money. Anyway I nudge an American next to me and ask him if he understands what they are asking of me. He assures me he does not but suggests that I let him take his choice of currency and coins so I, in desperation, gesticulate to him to take his choice. To this day I do not know if I was gypped.

Anyway I soon get on to counting money because I realized I couldn't afford many funny experiences. When I returned to the car and presented the papers, Mae had worked herself into a lather explaining that on one of the papers they had miscalculated and written <u>Negro.</u> Upon further investigation among ourselves we finally solved the problem which meant black the color of our car! This was one of the hottest days I ever felt, practically everybody on the bridge was soaked with perspiration.

At last we are across and instantly you realize you are in a different country. At first we felt unprotected and alone in fact horribly so even though we had laughed about bandits, being robbed, etc. We drove to Monterrey, a distance of 146 miles thru scorching winds that fairly blistered our faces. Although we had made a feeble attempt to air-condition our car with dry ice purchased in Laredo—there really was not enough although 'tis all the ice cream factory could spare us. We had expected to drive much further than Monterrey but the delay at the international bridge threw us off. Hotel accommodations after you leave Monterrey are far apart and even scarce if you arrive after 4:00 PM, so our guide book said, which we were consulting constantly; so we realized it would be unwise to pass this place up after 3:30 PM. So here it is we make our first attempt to buy gasoline in Mexico. After much gesticulating and maneuvering we finally put it over and purchased 50 liters, then set forth to try to locate the central part of the city and locate ourselves... This means that all business places are closed.

There are heavy iron grills over all windows on residences and businesses and during siesta time there are heavy shutters to completely obstruct the view, so window shopping is not so popular in Mexico. As we drove along the streets of Monterrey in search of a hotel I must admit I was disappointed. The heat was oppressive, the city deserted and I was tired. So we came to the Monterrey Hotel and registered. There we found it quite modern. After we were located and had a bath we were again ready to set forth to see what was to be seen. Across the street from our hotel we found an English speaking youth of about 16 years of age who served as guide for us.

After a lovely dinner at the   - Hotel we took an old horse drawn carriage for a moonlit tour of the city. This proved most delightful since we went into all the byways and hedges, our young guide being very efficient explaining all buildings and points of interest to us. After we had dismissed our carriage we walked through the thieves market.   This was truly a revelation. I feel sure Old India has nothing on this. Once when I hesitated when some food was being cooked over come coals, our guide urged me on, explaining that he was afraid I was going to buy some and I must not because the meat was unborn calf which would probably be offensive to me.

The following day found us still exploring Monterey rather than being off; we visited the various tile factories, the brewery, and the penitentiary. The latter place causing my friend, Mae Jones, (who boasts of having no fear of any thing) to quake in her boots and insist upon leaving. Late in the afternoon we took a very beautiful but decidedly the most dangerous drive of our entire trip up on Mt. Chipenqua.

The shops in Monterrey are just as lovely as anywhere in Mexico. You will find practically anything there and the prices are just as good. After a complete survey of everything we had fallen in love with this city so stayed over another night. The people there are delightful and quite understanding in case you can make them understand at all. Reluctantly on July 3 we moved on toward Mexico City. We passed thru some marvelous farming country where cattle raising seemed to predominate. Shortly after leaving Monterrey we passed a motor cop; he rode with us for about 100 miles. In the meanwhile we had stopped and had conversation with him twice, such as it was, his English was almost as poor as our Spanish, but he tried so hard to make himself pleasant and helpful. In fact we found this characteristic of all Mexicans. We drove 319 miles on in our second day in Old Mexico. We had Cuidad Valles as our destination and though it was only about 4:30 when we reached there, we decided to remain for the night. "Twas raining and the narrow streets were muddy and altogether very uninviting. We took turns about inspecting the hotels and making reservations so this happened to be my turn. There was very little to choose from and night so close on we felt ourselves lucky to find anything. There was no lobby in front; you walked directly into the dining room from the street. It was fairly attractive all done in red, black, and ivory with lovely velour chairs thru out. These were hand made. The proprietor was exactly what you'd expect a Mexican bandit to look like—dark, with keen black eyes, a goatee, and in fact all accessories for a typical bandit. We looked at the rooms, all the best had already been taken so what we had to take resembled penitentiary cells very much, built on the inside with hallways on both sides, iron bars over the windows which faced the hall with no way to shut off the view. This was discouraging but there were so many nice Americans here we didn't feel at all afraid. Supper in the dining room was abominable. We slept very little. There was so much confusion all night—Once I called to Dorothy and asked her what she thought they were doing downstairs. She says "Oh probably just a little murder contest. I imagine our proprietor will be victorious." When we had first registered he had stroked his goatee and boasted of having opened and operated his hotel for ten days without an assault. We had tried supper in the dining room without success, pushed our food back and got up hungry. Kate in desperation for food had eaten a few bites and became horribly nauseated, so we were glad when daylight came and we could be off. Without breakfast this was our third meal we were minus. The drive of 67 miles from here to Tamayenchale? was delightful. Vegetation was green and fresh looking, the cattle were sleek. At Tamayenchale in the greenest little place in Mexico, we took some time off here and inspected all the little shops, markets, schools and churches. One church here was over 400 years old.

When we parked for gas here the natives surrounded us smiling and trying hard to say something. They brought the gas out in tin measures and again we had to do a lot of maneuvering to make a settlement. 'Twas here on leaving this little place at the foot of the mountain we saw our first orchids growing wild!

From here on to Mexico City we ascended and descended these perfectly marvelous mountains you've heard so much about. The grade is not over 6% and the views are positively breath-taking. I probably have omitted one of the most impressive things on the trip when I have not mentioned the natives with their burros along the highway. You do not see any wagons or buggies? these people made. Transportation is exactly the same as it has been for 100's of years—just the same little patient burros loaded to the gill with fresh corn stalks, wood or what have you all tied carefully and securely on his back with sometimes nothing visible but his meek little face. It is indeed depressing to think that down thru the ages there is so little of any evidence of progression. We could not help but wonder as we drive slowly if and when what this highway will do toward modernizing that country. Alas! We look at our watches and find it is 3:00 PM—thus making the fourth meal missing. What shall we do for by this time we are beginning to feel we should not have been so choosy when suddenly it dawns upon some member of the party that on June 29 as we drove into Laredo, Texas we purchased some cheese and Ritz crackers, so with renewed courage we stop the car and get out to locate this feast in the trunk of our car. In getting out on this mountain top, we are surprised to find it's really cold even tho it is July 4. We are forced to put on our coats. Now this is something as we eat we hear strange tongues in a strange land. Upon looking around we see flocks of sheep and their shepherds far away on other mountain sites, probably being corralled into their fold for the night. In the meanwhile a Mexican truck driver passes and sees we are having some difficulty about closing the trunk on the car. He gallantly assists, then with a smile is off. Often during this particular day before we had thoughts of the cheese and crackers I had threatened to get out and tap a cactus. As you no doubt already know the cactus serves as their food, drink, and for many other purposes even to make their huts.

Our first stop after <u>luncheon</u> is when we pass an old cemetery. There is a burial going on so we park our car and attend. This may seem a bit uncalled for but we decided that so long as we were doing Mexico we might as well make it 100%. Several miles outside Mexico City we got into a traffic jam, caused from the road celebrations. They really are proud of this highway because while Mexico means very little to us, we mean everything to them - and they are glad of the connection. Outside Mexico City the rural people we saw on the highway were exactly like the mental pictures I've always had of Jerusalem's people during Christ's lifetime. All the women had shawls drawn closely around their heads, even tho most of them were barefoot. The men all wore serapes and heavy leather sandals.

Anyway we finally got into the city and located very comfortably in our hotel. Kate is still sick from the abominable supper the night before and can't eat so Mae dines in our hotel while Dorothy and I set off elsewhere. After a long brisk walk we find ourselves in Sanborn's which seems to be quite popular with Americans. 'Tis here we have our first meal in Mexico City. Upon leaving we find most everything's closed. We wanted to buy some cards so we hailed a taxi, told him what we wanted, then afterwards to our hotel. He nodded as tho he understood quite well. After riding for many miles we began to get suspicious. I never have known just what he meant but finally decided he was stalling for time trying to decide where we wanted to go. After so long we took a postcard from a bag and explained that was what we wanted so the next thing we knew he landed us at the Post Office! --which of course was closed about 1:30 PM. 'Twas around 2:15 PM when we got the cards and got back to our hotel. The following day was Sunday—we planned to see a bull fight. Part of the crowd attended church Sunday morning and 4:00 PM found us all at the arena for the fight. This proved to be positively blood curling! After very colorful preliminaries where the most beautiful girls parade in open cars and carriages and lovely horses with their riders keep time to the music and many other things, there comes the ghastly bull fight. I shall not go into the details except to say that 6 magnificent bulls were mutilated within two hours. After leaving this arena we went to our hotel for wraps, then set forth for the Imperial Palace, where a tea was being staged in honor of the delegates to the Official Opening of the Pan American Highway. This was by far the prettiest thing any of us had ever seen. It would be difficult for me to put it in to any words. The food was marvelous even tho it was all Mexican and we failed to recognize anything. Beautiful corsages of rosebuds were given all the ladies. After the banquet the guests were entertained with native dances and music. Over the terrace of this lovely old palace motion pictures were taken of everything. The Palace was started by the Aztecs when Maximillan was ruler. He completely re-furnished and remodeled it. Evidently he ruled in gorgeous splendor. The present President Cordinos does not occupy the Palace. He prefers not to since he is a common man and never entertains. All the people of Mexico seem to love him dearly.

On Monday we tried to contact our representative, Josephus Daniels. I had a letter of introduction from Senator Joe T. Robinson; he was out and we failed to see him so we did not make any further attempts. On Tuesday we visited the National Palace. This proved interesting but for some reason Mae Jones developed a terrible headache and had to turn in for the night. I imagine trying to understand the broken English of our guide had something to do with it. Anyway Dorothy and I stepped off again late at night in quest of food. We decided to try a place recommended by the AAA Club which is supposed to be famous for its seafoods. The menu is all in Spanish and we can't make anything of it. Finally a young man at another table realizes our predicament and makes a feeble stab at rescuing us. We find him to be of very little help. We are trying to find soft shelled crabs so we draw a picture; neither of us being skilled artists. He mistook it for octopus and was on the verge of serving some when we, with our cunning, got on to it and objected. Then he takes us to the kitchen refrigerator and various things. We are still no better off since we do not recognize any of the dishes. So we tell them to shoot something, anything. This proved only fair, but quite a nice experience.

We met a young College professor from the University of New Mexico. He was staying at the same hotel where we were and had brought a flock of girls down for some extension courses. They had about given him the air so he sorta joined forces with us. He spoke Spanish fluently so this was quite an asset to our group. He went shopping with us and did all the bickering. On Wednesday we took our car and drove to an old Carmelite monastery called The Desert of the Lions built in 1606. This is located on a mountain at an altitude of 9000 feet. 'Twas around 1:30 PM when we were there and the thermometer stood around 60 degrees. A young Mexican boy took us through this monastery. There are many strange underground passages and torture chambers. Each of us were given candles. We inspected these carefully and asked a million questions. Once when Dr. Comfer laughed we asked him what the guide had said who spoke only Spanish. He had told the professor that he spoke pretty good Spanish for a Gringo. This was funny since Dr. Comfer prided himself on speaking it perfectly. The drive thru the most beautiful fir forest, the professor wore his overcoat while the ladies shivered. On going back into the City we had lunch at Tacuba, a restaurant famous for its Mexican food done in style. I believe this was about the most immaculate eating place we saw. I shall never forget the green sauce over the chicken. We thought sure it would kill us but by this time I guess we had built up a great resistance, anyway we seemed to flourish on it!....."

The rest of May Cole's Journal is unavailable.

If you had the pleasure of knowing May Cole, you will remember this saying which she loved to quote:

When I was young my shoes were red

And I could kick way over my head

Then I was married and my shoes were white

And I could dance far into the night.

Now I'm old and my shoes are black

I can hardly walk to the gate and back

But I can sit in the corner and grin

And think of the wonderful places I've been.

May Templin Cole died January 3, 1988 and is buried in Oak Hill Cemetery with her Husband, William.

Amazing Attalla,

Alabama

From Her Front Porch Swing at 422 Fifth Avenue - Vivian Mae Brown Jones

"I was born May 6, 1898 on Fifth Avenue, Attalla, Alabama named Vivian Mae Brown after Vivian Lamont Nicholson, my Mother's youngest brother, and a school teacher "Mae" whom my Mother loved.

No one ever had more loving parents - devoted to their two children. Ralph Bradford (who later called himself James Ralph because he wanted his initials to be J̲ames R̲alph Brown as our Father was called Jim Brown.)

My Mother, Hattie F. Brown as a girl was Harriet Nicholson named for one of her Father's Sisters but she always signed her name Hattie F̲. Brown.

I was born in a two story yellow house on West Fifth Avenue, I do not remember except my Father bought 150 feet across the street - a small house but my Grandmother Nicholson died here. (Small house was turned around and moved to the back of the lot facing the alley) New house was

33

built facing West Fifth Avenue and this house continues as 422 West Fifth Avenue.

Going to the bathroom meant going down the steps and to the garden. Getting a drink of water meant putting a bucket down into a well and getting water to drink with, cook with, wash clothes—any water we had.

My Father, James Richard Brown came from Ohatchee, Calhoun County, and Ragland, Alabama. My father's early days were full of sorrow losing a wife and three children-two small - maybe from whooping cough, - his wife, Mamie Henderson died at the birth of their third child - Mother and baby being buried in the same grave in Ohatchee, Alabama.

One first memory is my Father spanking my hand - He was busy talking business to another- was telling me to go away - wait. I was very hurt - cried - I can't remember that my Father ever scolded me again. In fact my Father waited 20 years before he married a second time - had said he would never marry again. I truly say our Father let us have what we wanted and I admit he spoiled us.

Very happy days I had going to Sunday School across town - still on Fifth Avenue, the early Methodist church there as well as my Grandparents Benjamin Harrison Nicholson and I could go over the fence from school, get to hot corn bread for my lunch. My grandmother had lived in Lebanon - died in 1911. Then my grandfather died at another daughter (who was my Aunt Annie) just five miles away in Gadsden, Alabama. We always felt my Grandfather died of grief - didn't want to leave home (thought Mollie would return but Grandpa had a stroke, only weeks after Grandma died - both buried in Oakhill Cemetery, Attalla. Add. Benjamin Harrison Nicholson at 18 had a horse and rode in the Calvary with first Joe Wheeler and then General Bedford Forest when Emma Sansom (rode on the back of his horse), told General Forest where the ford was in the creek and the group escaped the Union soldiers who were following them to Rome, Georgia. Just west of Rome, Ga. General Forest tricked the Union Commander, Col. Streight, into believing that the Confederate soldiers were more numerous and would capture them. He had the same men carry different battle flags as they rode in a circle around the Yankees. The Yankees surrendered.

The name Attalla means "My Home." Indians lived here, the peaceful Cherokees - we have <u>Coosa</u> River, <u>Etowah</u> High School: Counties, Cities, Rivers all over the state have Indian names.

I went to grammar school in a frame building - I loved each teacher, friends were great - games like Pop the Whip we played at recess. Then I graduated from Etowah County High School in 1914, just 5 in my class. I am the last one living having gone this year to my 75th Reunion (1989) - on May 6 I was 91 years old and my one daughter, Martha Lou, having a 50th High School Reunion.

My father did not want me to go to Montgomery Woman's College (only four years old) nor to Athens College because a student there had died of typhoid fever the year before. So the choice was Randolph Macon Woman's College in Lynchburg, Virginia and I continue to thank my parents for giving me the Vita Abundante four years. I feel RMCS stands out all over the United States. My Father didn't live to see me graduate (1918) - dying in 1917.

My Father and his brothers (Watt and Adolphus Brown) were shrewd business men, bought land, with A. L. DuPre near Wesson bridge on Big Wills Creek - owned the Dam, developed Etowah Light and Power Company which later was bought by Col. Lay (who had originally sold the land to them) and thus was one of four companies incorporated as Alabama

Power Company. We did have the first electric stove in the county in the early twentieth century.

By 1912 my Father built a two story house at 422 West Fifth Avenue. In front was a railroad spur which brought lumber from my Father's Farm - a short way out of town. The Farm sold for a portion of Camp Sibert in the Second World War.

A grist mill was burned to the ground –Heading Mills in Attalla, Blountsville and Armuchee, Ga. meant income to us as well as Land - building of Attalla First (frame) Post Office on Third Street first belonged to my Father. Now we have a new brick Attalla Post Office on the corner of downtown Fourth Street.

My brother Ralph also was a wise business man - went to Howard College (Now Samford in Birmingham, AL) and played football. Had first dry cleaning plant in Attalla and had the vision for a Motor Court - Brown's Motor Court still in operation but under another name.

Ralph Brown was very special to his wonderful family but lived to be only 49 years old (Doctors in Birmingham, AL never explained his death following an operation for gall bladder.) His wife, Kate Wise Brown was outstanding in her friendship with me and their daughters Elaine (Mrs. Hayden Ford), Katherine Mae Burke (my namesake) (Mrs. Louie Burke), and Harriet (Mrs. Bill Burke) and their families have blessed me in many ways.

I went by train to go to College - we never had a car, so I chose a young man, Clarence Foster Jones who in 1919 had a car and a good job with the Railroad. My Mother said she could not live alone so Clarence and I started living upstairs at 422 W. Fifth Avenue. My Mother lived only five years longer and died in 1923 after my father had died in 1917.

Clarence Jones didn't want to be transferred to South Alabama so he bought a small plumbing place down the street from where we lived. Drug stores sold gasoline. Clarence, too, wanted to buy land so we bought next door on the corner and built in 1925 a two story brick duplex and a one story brick duplex with space for four cars (one for each apartment) in-between. This means that I still live on at 422 W Fifth Avenue but walking days are almost over."

Written in 1989 at age 91.   VMBJ

Vivian Mae Brown Jones lived at 422 Fifth Avenue, Attalla, Alabama until she died on February 17, 1994 at the age of 95.

Who Turned On the Lights in Attalla?

Chief Researcher: Katherine Mae Brown Burke

Reference : Gadsden Courthouse   From Deed Record Book I - I , page 204

Reference: The Gadsden Times, Sunday, June 27, 1982 by Jackie Harris, Times Staff Writer

The hero is Captain W. P. Lay (later Col. W. P. Lay) who was born in Cedar Bluff, Alabama and was a Riverboat Captain on the Coosa River. From the Alabama Review July 1951 page 193 " Capt. William Patrick Lay was born in 1853, the son of Capt. Cummins Lay and a grandson of Capt. John Lay, pioneers in flatboat river transportation on the Coosa before the coming of the steamboats. Capt. William Patrick, a licensed pilot, was financially interested in the Alabama II. He is best known as the father of The Alabama Power Company and was its first president. His plan to produce hydro-electricity was copied not only by The United States but by the whole civilized world. Lay Dam on the Coosa River stands as a monument to his achievements, and a tablet of enduring bronze proclaims him as benefactor of his fellow man."

Col. Lay was intrigued with the power of the river and believed that hydro electric power could be used to operate a generator so that electric power could produce electricity. For his experiment he found Wesson's Mill on Big Wills Creek west of Attalla.

To quote from the History of Attalla by George P. Walker, III found on the Internet.

"In the fall of 1902, Captain William Patrick Lay, of Gadsden, began construction of a small hydro electric generating plant at the site of Wesson Mill on Big Wills Creek, just southwest of Attalla. The plant was constructed, in Lay's words, "First to supply the City of Attalla with electricity; second, to pump water into a tall stand pipe which would furnish Attalla with water, and third, to demonstrate the possibilities and economy of hydro electric power for which I had been contending for a number of years preceding. When the plant was completed, a line was strung from the 75-horsepower turbine - driven generator, over the mountain to a light on a pole in the heart of Attalla. Captain Lay himself threw the switch, bringing electricity to the community."

And to continue the story: Captain Lay had proved that electric power could be produced by water. He set in motion a plan using the water of the Coosa River and constructing high dams for large scale hydro and steam generating plants which became the foundation on which the Southern Company system of integrated power companies is based today." Hallelulah!

But that isn't all. To continue the story....

Captain Lay had been successful with his experiment on Big Wills Creek so his interest returned to the big water of the Coosa River for the hydro electric possibilities of large dams and big power. He sold the Wesson Mill property in Attalla in November 1904 to A.L. Dupre and wife, J. R. Brown and wife and Adophus Brown and wife, all of Attalla, who on the 4th day of November 1904 formed a corporation, The Etowah Light and Power Company. The plot thickens. (Now we see how Attalla and three families fit in the big picture.) In the Courthouse in Gadsden, Alabama see Deed Record Book I-I Page 204.

Etowah Light and Power Company operated until 1915 when Captain Lay purchased the corporation to become the fourth company under an umbrella as The Alabama Power Company.

"And that isn't all!"

To continue from George P. Walker III's History of Attalla "to enlist the support of Attalla in the Big Wills Creek project, Captain Lay, at the request of Etowah Light and Power Company, agreed that the schools of Attalla would **FOREVER** have free electricity and to this day, schools and other city buildings have two meters—one for free lights for the schools and another for billed service."

Also from George P. Walker's History of Attalla---"Did you know that Attalla was the first US City to have electric street lights and was also the birthplace of Alabama Power Company." Recently in 2003 signs have appeared on the highways entering Attalla announcing

Attalla, The Birthplace of Electricity in Alabama.

So the mystery is solved "Who Turned on the Lights in Attalla" Answer Captain W. P. Lay with the help of Etowah Light and Power Company and three Attalla families. We who live now in Attalla as well as others who remember, are eternally grateful.

Mystery Solved!!!!!

From Deed Record Book

Gadsden Court House Book I-I page 204

This indenture made this 4th day of Nov. 1904, between A. L. DuPre and Wife, S.J. DuPre, J.R. Brown and Wife, Hattie Brown, and Aldophus Brown and Wife, L.M.Brown, parties of the first part and the ETOWAH LIGHT AND POWER COMPANY, a corporation party of the second part, Witnesseth, that A. L. DuPre and wife one of the parties of the first part in consideration of the issuance to him of Forty-five shares of the capitol stock of said company, party of the second part, and J.R. Brown and wife, another party of the second part in consideration of the issuance to him of Forty-five shares of the capital stock of said company party of the second part, do each hereby grant, bargain, sell and convey unto the said party of the second an undivided one fourth interest in the herein below described real estate and Adophus Brown and wife the other party of the first part in consideration of the issuance to him of ninety-shares of the capital stock of the company, party of the second part, do hereby grant bargain sell and convey unto the said party of the second part one undivided one half interest in and to the following real estate and easements to-wit+

Ten acres in the North east corner of fraction thirteen (13) of section. Twenty-seven (27) on which is located the new

41

dam and power house recently constructed by W. P. Lay also fraction twenty two (22) of section twenty-seven and all that part of Fraction twelve (12) of section twenty-seven lying south of Big Wills creek (except one acre on the east side of the said fraction twelve reserved by J.H. Wesson said acre not here sold is on the north side of the Public road and on the east side of the proposed mill race also excepted the mineral interest in Fraction twenty two of said section) also one undivided interest in all that part of fraction thirteen (13) of section twenty-seven (27) lying east or in the bend on the east side of Big Wills creek and all of the above described land being in section twenty seven(27) township (11) range (5) east in Etowah County Alabama together with the dam, power house and all buildings and improvements thereon and containing about ninety acres more or less. Also the rights to back water and maintain same up to the seventeen foot level (as surveyed) covering lands owned by J.H. Wesson in section twenty-three(23) in township (11)eleven range five (5) east also the right to back water unto the seventeen (17) foot level as surveyed over the lands along both sides of Big Wills Creek where the same crosses any land owned by Roland Brothers in section twenty three (23) and twenty six (26) township eleven (11) range five east also all the rights privileges and easments acquired by Laura J. Lay under the petition filed by her in the Probate Judges office of Etowah County, Alabama, April the 28th. 1904, the verdict of the Jury and the 28th, 1904, the verdict of the Jury and the decrees condeming the land to be covered or overflowed by the construction of the dam on the said above land and all the rights obtained in said proceedings are hereby conveyed and all of said rights and easments being in Etowah County Alabama, and all of the said lands and rights and easments herein conveyed being the same property on the ...(unable to read on fold of paper)

All of said consideration herein named amounting in the aggregate to one hundred and eighty shares of stock of the par value of one hundred dollars each and making eighteen thousand dollars and the receipt of all of which is hereby acknowledged. To have and to hold said above described land and easments to the said Etowah Light and Power Company, party of the second part and to its representatives and assigns forever. And that A. L. DuPre and J. R. Brown two of the parties of the first part will forever warrant and defend the title to each a undivided one fourth interest in said land and easments to the said party of the second part and to its representatives and assigns from every lawful claim whatsoever, And the said Aldophus Brown the other part of the first part will forever warrant and defend the title to the other one undivided one half interest in and to the said land and easments to the said party of the second part and to its representatives and assigns from every lawful claim whatsoever. In testimony whereof the parties of the first part have signed and sealed these presents on the day above written.....J.R.Brown, Hattie Brown,A.L.DuPre, S.J. Dupre Aldophus Brown, L.M.Brown Witness by I, S. W. Johnson, a Notary Public in and for said county State of Alabama, Etowah County...who are known to me acknowledged before me on this day that being informed of the contents of the conveyance, they executed the same voluntarily on the day the same bears date. Given under my hand and seal this the 4th day of November 1904.....S.W. Johnston...Notary Public

****

Copied from the program of the dedication of the first power dam on the Coosa River known as Lock and Dam No. 12

"About this time, 1902, Captain Lay first became engaged in the production of electric energy by water power. He rebuilt a dam at an old mill site on Big Wills Creek near Attalla, installing a 100 horsepower capacity turbine driven generator. Satisfying himself as to the feasibility of generating electricity by water power, he sold the plant a year or two later to Adolph and Jim Brown, of Attalla. It was afterwards owned by Alabama Power Company ..."

"With Earl Lay, his son, and Oliver R. Hood, his attorney, both of Gadsden, he organized Alabama Power Company on December 4, 1906, with an initial capitalization of $5,000. The Company's charter was filed with Hon. J. W. Penn, Judge of Probate, in the old Etowah County courthouse, since destroyed. Lands were then acquired by Captain Lay at the site selected by Government engineers for Lock and Dam No. 12 and at other locations, and thereafter he obtained the passage through Congress of an act approved by the President on March 4, 1907, authorizing the erection of a dam across the Coosa at Lock 12 of such height as the Chief of engineers and Secretary of War might approve."

City Of Attalla School System Receives Free Electricity For Lights

A franchise negotiated over eighty years ago places the City of Attalla and its school system in an enviable position. They don't have to pay for electricity for lights. Pg. 10 The Gadsden Times Sunday June 27, 1982

The franchise, a form of contract, was signed by Attalla forefathers on March 5, 1915, and Alabama Power Company officials, and is still in effect today.

Who were the forefathers responsible for negotiating this contract? They were: J.R. Brown, grandfather of Mrs. Louie C. Burke, and Mrs. Kenneth Riddle of Rome, Georgia; Adolphus Brown, brother of J.R.Brown; and A.L.DuPre, grandfather of Tom Banks.

In 1904, these three men had purchased from Col. W.P. Lay the dam at the old mill on Big Wills Creek near Attalla where Lay had installed a 100 horsepower capacity turbine-driven generator that produced electricity by water.

While Lay was occupied with organizing the Alabama power on the Coosa River, the Browns and DuPre formed the

45

Etowah Light and Power Company which produced electricity for Attalla until March 6, 1915.

At this time there were several other light and power producing companies in Alabama which all agreed to merge with Alabama Power. Etowah Light and Power would agree only if there was a stipulation in the deed to allow Attalla to have free electricity for the schools. This was agreed to, and is the reason the Attalla City School system has free electricity for light today.

I have been interested in researching this information for many years for two reasons. First, Aunt Mae Brown Jones, daughter of J. R. Brown, often talked about our family involvement and the fact that the family was given the first electric stove in Etowah County. Second, my son, Brad Burke, is an environmental engineer with Southern Company, the holding company for Alabama Power.

I have a copy of the Lay Dam Dedication Program in which there is a paragraph explaining the Brown involvement.

We are grateful that Alabama Power Company has recently (2003) awarded Attalla, Alabama $8500.00 for the placement on Highway U.S. 11 two signs: "Welcome to Attalla, Alabama. Birthplace of Alabama Power Company."

Researched by Katherine Brown Burke

Gadsden, Alabama

Headlines page 10 The Gadsden Times, Sunday June 27, 1982

City of Attalla
School System Receive Free Electricity for Lights

By Jackie Harris, Times Staff Writer

"A franchise negotiated nearly 70 years ago places the City of Attalla and its school system in a unique, enviable position. They don't have to pay for electricity for lights.

The franchise, a form of a contract, was signed May 5, 1913 by Attalla's forefathers and Alabama Power Co. (APC) officials. It still is in effect, providing the Attalla City Hall, jail and schools not only an impressive savings each month, but also the city a franchise fee which the company annually pays in all areas APC is located.

Ed Crosby, the APC spokesman, said that earlier this year Alabama Power paid a franchise fee of $95,279.60 to the City of Attalla. And to give an idea of the savings the city's school system reaps as a result of the franchise, Crosby said that for 1981, the electricity bill for lighting alone would have been $46,303.94.

It all started as early as 1902 when steamboat Captain William P. Lay, a Cherokee County native built the first hydro-electric plant at Wesson Mill on Big Wills Creek near Attalla..... The article continues for 2 full columns.

Memories

BY Katherine Mae Brown Burke

I was born on October 26, 1925, and was given the name Katherine Mae Brown. My mother was Kate Wise Brown, and my father was James Ralph Brown. My mother's parents were William Randolph Wise and Lula Mae Croft Wise. My father's parents were James Richard Brown, and Hattie F. Brown. My father had one sister, Vivian Mae Brown Jones.

We lived in the 600 block of Hughes Avenue in Attalla. There were no houses in front of us, but we had a beautiful view from our screened in porch of the foothills of the Appalachian Mountains and Little Wills Creek. Little Wills Creek meandered around our block and crossed Fifth Avenue. Sometimes the creek would overflow its banks on Fifth Avenue. On occasions certain churches would hold baptisms there. Later a bridge was built.

There was also a railroad trestle over the creek. Groups of us had fun walking the trestle and swimming in the creek.

Also in front of our house was a street car track. On many occasions I would place straight pins on the track, and after the street car would pass over them, to my delight, the pins were formed into a perfect pair of miniature scissors. At some point in time the track was either removed or paved over.

To the left of our house was the home of the Landers, and to the right was a vacant lot on which the Frank Ledbetters build their home. Beside their home was a family known as the Weems. In later years the Ed Smiths built a lovely brick home on the corner to the left of our house. There were three houses across the street to the left of the front of our house, home of the Washburns, and the Lees. I can't remember who lived in the third home.

Today, all the homes are gone because Ramada Inn purchased the land in the seventies, and built an Inn which today is the Econo Lodge. My mother's magnolia still stands there.

Fifth Avenue was behind our house, and another railroad ran beside Fifth Avenue. My earliest memory is of mother getting me to bed before dark, and as I viewed a picture on the wall of my bedroom, I could hear the lonely sound of a train whistle as the train went by.

I had two sisters, Lawrence Elaine Brown and Harriet Wise Brown. I remember Dad had built for us a playhouse in the back yard. It was furnished with a toy stove, refrigerator and table and chairs. The playhouse was so well constructed that when Elaine had her own home they were able to move it to her yard in East Gadsden. She married Hayden Ford, and they had two children, Hayden Ford, Jr., and Rebecca Elaine Ford. Harriet married Bill Burke, brother of Louie C. Burke. They had three children: Cindy Burke, Betsy Burke, and Randy Burke, all of the above lived in Anniston, Alabama.

I attended first grade at the wooden school on first Street. I shall never forget my first grade teacher, Carrie Bell Norton. I studied piano with Helen Easley in a brick building nearby in which fourth, fifth, and sixth grades were taught. My class was the first to attend the new Attalla City School on Fourth Street. It was a beautiful building, and still stands today, though not occupied. The teachers I remember at this school were Mrs. Pilcher, Mrs. Helene Hinton, Elizabeth Griswald, and Louise Cole. I particularly remember Mrs. Louise Burke because she took our class on a field trip to the Coca-Cola plant in Gadsden.

In 1939 I attended Etowah High School. I was still taking piano lessons, this time from Mary D. Stewart. We had many music recitals.

While at Etowah, World War II began in 1941. Because of this event some of our activities were deeply affected. We were not allowed to have floats in a parade because of the need to conserve paper. Neither were we allowed to have a yearbook. This caused an inconvenience for our class even in later years.

In spite of the turmoil of the war years, the first marching band was organized. How proud everyone was to see them march down Main Street. For some reason I was voted to be a majorette. I played the flute.

My dear friends, Jane Banks Jenkins, and Lucy Turner Nowlin were always planning activities together. We would swim at Lake Rhea, attend church functions, and dances organized by Jimmy Wood, and Gordon Isbell. We called ourselves, "The Three Musketeers."

A chemical warfare camp was constructed near Attalla, and as a result a USO was organized in Attalla. Alice Ingram was hired to be the organizer and sponsor. On many occasions she would arrange a busload of girls with a chaperone (Mrs. Logsdon) to go to events where many soldiers from Camp

Sibert would go. As long as Mrs. Logsdon was chaperone, mother let me participate in this war effort.

I was a member of the Beta Club, and would attend meetings in Birmingham. At one meeting, I was elected state secretary.

Sometimes, after school or on weekends, Marion Harris Millican and I would rent a horse, and go horseback riding. We both had fun.

Upon graduation in 1943, my family and I decided that I would attend Sullins Junior College in Bristol, Tennessee/ Virginia. It was a girls' school, and the students were from all over the United States. My roommate was Sally Thorup from Wellesley Hill, Massachusetts.

During the second year at Sullins, Sally's boyfriend, Bushnell Welch, who was a pilot in the Air Force was reported missing in action. Before our graduation, he was located and returned to the U.S. They were to be married in the summer, and I was asked to be in the wedding. After graduation, I went with Sally to Wellesley, and was there for a month. Sally's family invited me to stay in Massachusetts and attend school at Wellesley College. I was very tempted to stay because I loved the area, but mother said, "Come Home."

While at home the summer in 1945, I took a course in learning to teach Visual Method Music at the encouragement of Gladys Freeland. Several others in the Gadsden area took this course also. I taught this method in the Attalla City School, and other schools also. It was quite an interesting course.

In the fall of 1945, I attended the University of Alabama, and while there joined the Alpha Gamma Delta Sorority. At the time, there were very few men on campus. The previous summer I had started dating Louie C. Burke, who had returned home from World War II as a navigator in the Air Force. He chose Auburn University to finish his college work in engineering. We saw each other on several occasions during our college days.

We were married June 12, 1948, at the First Methodist Church in Attalla. Tillman Sprouse conducted the ceremony.

August 5, 1949, our daughter, Patricia Harriet Burke was born. We were living in the "Brown House" at 111 Hughes Avenue and later moved to an apartment behind my mother and father's home at 609 Hughes Avenue. We planned to build a house in East Gadsden near Louie's work with Allis-Chalmers. The house was almost completed when I was expecting our second child. I went to the hospital from Attalla on April 23, 1953, and we became the proud parents of a 9 pound, 10 oz. Baby boy whom we named James Bradford Burke. The new house was completed except for the yard. Thank goodness for mother, Pearl, and Louie. Due to all their help, we managed to move. I have often said "that's the only way I could have left Attalla."

We had many happy years together at 131 Penn Drive, Gadsden, Alabama. Louie worked at Allis-Chalmers as a manager of Manufacturing Engineering. The company later sold to a German Company, and was called Siemens-Allis. Today it is known as Siemens. After the children were older, in 1964, I applied for a teaching job in the Gadsden City School System, and taught at Litchfield Jr. High School (later Litchfield High School) until 1984.

In 1980 we moved to 107 Cleveland Court in downtown Gadsden, Alabama. We enjoyed our years at this address until 1989, when Louie was diagnosed with prostate cancer. He was a loving husband and wonderful father.

Our daughter, Patricia, lives in Guntersville, Alabama, and is Librarian at Guntersville High School. She is married to Kerry Jackson, who is the owner of WGSV-AM and WTWX-FM radio stations. She has three sons, Drew, Brett, and Clay. Drew lives in Birmingham. He has a wife, Haley, and a daughter, Burkely. Drew is a project manager in the E-commerce department of AmSouth Bank, and Haley is an account executive with AL.com. Brett lives in Guntersville, and works with the Berry Group. His wife, Sarah, is employed with Carlton Cove in Huntsville. Clay is presently attending Snead State Community College, Boaz, Alabama, on an Academic Scholarship.

Our son, Brad, lives in Birmingham and is employed by Southern Company as an Environmental engineer. His wife, Maria, is also employed at Southern Company as a Chemical Engineer. They have two children, Jeff, age 6, and Jamie, age 3.

My father, J. Ralph Brown, was the son of Jim and Hattie Brown, who were pioneers and contributed much to building the City of Attalla. Jim Brown with his brother, Adolpus, and A.L. DuPre operated the first Electric Power Plant (Etowah Light and Power Company) in the city of Attalla.

My father was a graduate of Etowah High School, and until his death was a great supporter of the school. He played football at the school, and in his college days was an outstanding athlete. While at Howard College, (today Samford University) he scored the first touchdown made against the University of Alabama in Denny Stadium. His interest in sports extended through his business career, an avid Etowah High School football fan, and a member of the Quarterback Club.

With faith in the future of the City of Attalla, Mr. J. Ralph Brown began to operate Brown's Service Station in the year 1929 selling Red Hat gasoline. Several years later he built a new station across the street on North 4th Street where he handled Texaco products and serviced cars of all kinds.

It has been said that great men and women of our time have been those who visualized needs of the future, and prepared for those needs. During the years preceding World War II, Mr. and Mrs. J. Ralph Brown through their travels to other sections of our country where they saw many modern motels, visualized a need for this type of industry in North Alabama. With the idea in mind of the many people who traveled the highways through Attalla, Mr. Brown constructed twelve modern rooms on his business property, US. 278 and 431, and thus began "Brown's Motor Court." With the success of this undertaking he later added ten more rooms, a total of twenty two, and a restaurant building. At his time the Motor Court was the only one within a 75 mile radius. One might say that Kate and Ralph Brown were pioneers of the Motel Industry.

Some of the persons of note who have passed through the doors of Brown's Motor Court were the comedian Red Skelton, Jess Willard, one time heavyweight boxing champion, Eddie Hodges, movie star, and many other notables.

J. Ralph Brown was a member of The Methodist Church, and for years served on the Board of Stewards.

He was a Mason and a Shriner, and was active in community and civic work. He was a member of the Attalla City Council, Veteran of WWI, and was serving as Mayor Pro Tem at the time of his death.

He had planned to build a new motel where the present Holiday Inn is located, but this plan was discontinued because of his death in 1950 at the age of 49.

My dear sweet mother, Kate Brown, was always supportive of her husband. She continued to operate the motel after my father's death with the assistance of Claude Cagle, but after continuous operation of Brown's Motor Court and Service Station for 37 years , it was sold to W. A. McDaniel in the 1970s..

Kate Brown lived to be 95. She was a member of the First Methodist Church, and served on the Administrative Board. She was District President of WSCS (6 years,) president of the Pilot Club (1967-68, member of the Board of Directors of First national Bank, the Salvation Army Board and a number of other social and civic organizations.

Both Kate and Ralph Brown are buried in Oak Hill cemetery.

Memories of Attalla, Al.,

by Katherine Cole Frame

In 1920 when I was born in Attalla, Alabama on Hughes Avenue, there were no washing machines, no dial telephones, certainly no television, no Stouffers TV dinners, no ice makers in the "Ice Box," and men still tipped their hats when meeting a lady.

Our laundry or "washing" was picked up by Pauline Glass, niece of Anna Chandler, who was known as a superior laundress. She taught Pauline everything necessary about the art of laundering. Pauline got the clothes on Monday and brought them back on Thursday.

When Pauline married Roy Glass, my father and I went to the wedding. It was at Anna's house. Roy came to our house to wash the cars and sometimes drive me to school.

We moved from Hughes Avenue when I was about 4 to what we called "the little green house on E. Fifth Avenue." It was rented from Dr. Foreman and was down the street from my grandmother's house at 210 E. Fifth Avenue.

When I was 5 years old, my father had our house built at 209 E. Fifth Avenue - directly across the street from my grandmother's. To the left of my grandmother lived the Hutchinson family. Mrs. Hutchinson was an invalid and once, when my grandmother called on her, she had pointed to a spot on the wall and said "That thing has been spitting on me all day." There was a son named Norman and a daughter, Emma.

I believe Nettie was the name of the telephone operator. Her office was above Walker Drug Store on Fifth Avenue. I have heard my grandmother pick up the phone and say "Nettie, what does Charlie Cooper have today?" Charlie Cooper was our grocer in downtown Attalla. Mary Elizabeth and Charles were his children that I remember.

Next door to our house on Fifth Avenue lived Dr. Stewart, his wife, Theodosia, their son, Wycliffe, and Gene, Dr. Stewart's son by his first wife. When Dr. Stewart married Theodosia, she was a teacher at Nazareth College in Bardstown, Kentucky. Mrs. Stewart was from a distinguished background—born in Bardstown, in the house known as "The House of Three Governors." She was a lady of impeccable manners and a devoted friend to my family. Dr. Stewart called her "Dodo." Once when Mary French and her husband "French" were their guests for dinner, Mrs. Stewart had made her famous Beaten Biscuits, and French, confused as to the nomenclature, asked if the "Dodos" might be passed. Dr. Stewart was the doctor for the Attalla mines.

The ice truck would come in the morning on Mondays. We had signs to hang on the porch indicating how many pounds we wanted. The ice boxes were built somewhat like a refrigerator, and the huge chunk of ice went into a compartment at the top. When the ice truck came by, they scattered chips of ice on the road, and all of the children, including me, would follow, picking up the delicious delicacies. Once, we heard Wycliffe calling in his booming voice "twenty five pounds - we would take 50, but the mines are down." Wycliffe married a girl from Alfred,

New York. Her name was Amy. Jim O'Rear, upon hearing that Wycliffe had married a Yankee, said simply "Pity."

Mrs. Annie B. Johnson lived in a Victorian house across the street and up a way on the corner. Her husband, I believe, was a lawyer and had been dead for some time. She was very stately and she taught what we called then "Expression." I was one of her pupils. Her children were Rush, Lesane, and David, who was a great friend of Wycliffe Stewart. Mrs. Johnson's mother was Mrs. Rush. I remember Mrs. Rush as a dear, sweet person. I was at my grandmother's, who lived across the street, once when Mrs. Rush was there for a visit. I complained that something was in my eye, and she said "God will send a little tear and wash it away." When she went by train to California to visit relatives, she brought a small jar of black beach sand to me from the California beaches.

When my mother was a little girl at 210 E. Fifth Avenue, the Griders lived in the house later occupied by the Hutchinsons. There was a daughter called Bessie who later married Hosmer Price - the principal at the high school in Birmingham. The other daughter was Katherine, for whom I was named. She and Mother took a notion to build a raft. After working on it for week, they took it to Black Creek - where immediately after launching it sank to the bottom. Katherine was quick- witted and a bit of a free spirit. She won some sort of medal at school. One night out, she saw the teacher who awarded the medal, the teacher asked her why she didn't have it on, and Katherine replied, "Oh, that old thing?" and then quickly she continued on with "I never wear it at night." She died at 16 of spinal meningitis. About the time she won the medal, Etowah High School had a cheer that went as follows:

One a zip, two a zip

Three a zip zoy

Ziss boom firecracker

Phil ess moy.

Hip zoo, rah zoo

Hip zoo, boom

We're all from Etowah,

Give us room !!

Could it have been the precursor of Rap?

My neighborhood friends when I was growing up were Kenneth Riddle, Maxine and LaHolme McClendon, Paul Rogers and Jean his sister, George Hawkins, and then my cousin, Carolyn Norton. It was a real treat to be allowed to "play out" at night during the summer. We played old fashioned games like Drop the Handkerchief, London Bridge, and another one where one person said

"Bum, bum, bum, here we come." And the opposing player replied with

"where you from," then

"Pretty girls' station," and it continued on in this fashion,-- and maybe someone else will remember the rest of it. During "recess" at school we'd play "Pop the Whip" where everyone held hands and ran around and the ones on the end were virtually horizontal to the ground from the centrifugal force. Marbles was also a lot of fun, but it wasn't a girls' game. It was a wonderful time to be a child.

In downtown Attalla, there were two drug stores - Stewart's had a wonderful marble soda fountain. Leon Lochlear was the pharmacist, and I remember my Mother calling and asking "Leon, what is the medicine of the hour?" Outside was Mr. Hansard's popcorn stand, and a group of older boys, what we dubbed "drugstore cowboys," that would gather and sit around on a bench, and they were, as I remember, Goob Tarpley and Goofy Howell often there. Next door was Dryers Clothing Store and sometimes they would have a sign: GIVING UP covering their whole window, but at the bottom in tiny letters it would say "present stock."

My relatives were cousin Carolyn Norton, and her mother, "Aunt Bea," and more cousins, Dorothy and Louise Cole, who were Uncle Jess's children, and Sibyl Cole, Uncle Tommy's daughter, who lived up on sand Mountain. On my mother's side of the family were Cousin Carrie Lee and Cousin Myrtle, both Uncle Jake's children. Their children were Betty Lee and Jake Reams, and Carrie Lee and Bert Martin. I loved visiting them in Middlesboro, Ky. I still have pictures of Bert and Jake on their horses. They played for the polo team while at Culver Military Academy.

When I was about 12 my Father bought a pony for my birthday. His name was Dixie. My good friend Martha Lou Jones had a pony named Prince, and Dot Tarpley's pony was Nancy. The 3 of us spent many joyful times riding all over town and the surrounding countryside together. Once we rode out to Buddy Warren's farm where we somehow got into a fenced in area with a ferocious bull, but fortunately one of the hands who worked there got us out before any damage was done to us.

I have many happy memories of grammar school. The teachers I remember most were Mrs. Pilcher, Mrs. Guest, and Mary French. Mr. Clements was our principal. When he would visit our room, we would sing:

"How do you do Mr. Clements, how do you do?

Is there anything we can do for you?

We will do it if we can,

And stand by you like a man

How do you do Mr. Clements, how do you do?"

Scott, my son, wanted me to write about the Great Depression, but the impact of it really did not hit me until some years later. At the time, life just went on. I was 9 years old when Black Friday's stock market crash happened, when my parents were having a party. A man brought a cow to our house in payment for a debt to my father. We kept the cow for several years. A shed was built for her and she was milked in the morning and again at night by Claude, a Negro who lived in Fortwood. Sometimes when Claude would fall drunk, Daddy would drive all over Fortwood looking for someone who could come and milk Daisy. Once when he was desperately looking for anyone, my mother said "Stand back. I can milk the cow." She had remembered having a pet nanny goat as a child and had learned to milk her then. This would be a one time performance. Our icebox was soon overflowing with incredibly rich milk, so Mother sent milk every day to the grammar school, where there were children who needed it. No one worried about pasteurization, or the milk being homogenized, and no one suffered.

When the circus came to Gadsden, there would be a parade downtown on Broad Street with clowns, elephants, caged tigers, and sometimes glamorous girls riding the elephants. Miss Mae Jones, Martha Lou, and my mother and I went to watch the parade and stood on the side of the street with all of the crowd, almost within touching distance. Miss Mae, not wasting a precious moment, would be giving Martha Lou a spelling lesson. "Now spell tiger." We would be some of the fortunate children who went to the circus that night. Taylor Hardy told later of his father taking him to the parade and telling him that "he had been to the circus."

Men often came to our back door asking for something to eat. They were always white and very polite and not too shabbily dressed. They were simply looking for work and were down on their luck. If I happened to be alone in the house I would fix peanut butter and jam sandwiches. If one came after dark, he would get a good hot meal when our cook came back to fix dinner. I never felt too poor during the Depression, and my parents never talked about their lack of funds. They simply did what they could.

Louis Barrow lived in a rental house of my father's and I remember him coming to the back door to pay his rent. He had beautiful teeth and a million dollar smile. Even as a child I knew how to write a receipt and where the receipt book was kept. Louis Barrow was Joe Louis's uncle, and I believe Joe Louis's real name was Joe Barrow or Louis Barrow.

In Gadsden there was a colored nightclub called "The Royal Palm" and it was owned and operated by Jess Waller. Jess was Fats Waller's uncle and Fats came to Gadsden to perform there on occasion. "Ain't Misbehaving" featured a lot of his music and I've always missed it somehow, but I still want to see it.

Sepp Scales lived in a house on Third Street in Attalla. On Saturday nights she played the piano and entertained her friends. I remember that sometimes white people would park on the street just to listen.

Faye Keener was another good friend. Miss Ruby Sue was her mother. Bill Keener was her father. Charlotte and Billie were her sisters. Miss Ruby Sue had a wonderful trained voice and sang at many events and in the church choir. For a while she gave voice lessons to Faye and me. I don't remember if Faye showed any promise, but I was a complete failure. I believe Faye was the first officer in the women's branch of the Navy, called the WAVES in 1941. Paul Harvey announced it and my mother happened to be listening to the radio and heard the announcement.

My mother told of growing up with a girl named Mary Elgin Ventress. Her family was not financially well off, but her mother had the knack of sewing outfits and turning her out looking like a Town & Country model. She later married Mr. Beeman, of the Beeman Chewing Gum family.

Now I'll tell a little about a trip to New York in the summer of 1934. Martha Lou and her mother, Mae Jones, and my mother, May Templin Cole, and I motored to New York City in our Hudson, with wooden spoke wheels and spare tires on each side of the car. We took a picnic lunch for the first day, and we stayed in "tourist homes"- the Bed & Breakfasts of the day. While in New York we stayed at the Park Central Hotel. We ate at inexpensive places like The Automat, but we saw all the outstanding Broadway shows. I remember Alfred Lunt and Lynn Fontaine in "The Long Night" and Bob Hope in "Roberta." I still have some of the old play bills somewhere. I had dancing lessons from Agnes Boone at the Barbizon Hotel. There was a girl from Anniston in my class and she stayed up there and became a Rockette at Radio City Music Hall. We ran into Frank Jones, also from Anniston, and who had been one of my dancing teachers. Llewelyn Sikes was with Frank's group and had been Mary Muller's accompanist and maybe Frank's too. Anyway, when Miss Boone's accompanist left her, she was desperately looking for someone, and my mother suggested she try out Llewelyn. She did try out for the job and she got it.

Dudley Paul Frame, Jr was introduced to me by Miss Mae Jones in 1949, and we were married the following summer.

When Dudley went into the army, he was disappointed that he couldn't get into the Air Force because of color blindness. He had flying lessons after we had 3 children and he now is an instrument rated pilot, still passing his physical, and we fly many places in his Beechcraft Baron. We have lived in South Africa and Maracay, Venezuela and we visit San Miguel D'Allende in Mexico almost every year. He spent 3 years overseas in World War II beginning in North Africa fighting Rommell, was in the Normandy Invasion at Omaha Beach, and he was a clerk (Second Lieutenant) at the Anfa Conference in Casablanca, where he saw Churchill, Roosevelt, and Stalin.

We recently went to Attalla for the celebration of the 100th anniversary of the First Methodist Church, where I grew up. My mother had organized the Lavinia Hunter Sunday School class, so she would have a class to attend when I entered Sunday school. My grandfather was a contractor who built the church as a young man. His name was Maurice Hartselle Templin and he finished the church when he was 39 years old.

There were many old friends there – all the Walkers, the O'Rears, Julie Terrell, Steve McConnell, all the Isbells. Coleman and Lynn Howard were not there because they are Baptists, and I hope to see them soon.

We have lived in Anniston for 40 years.

When we couldn't find anyone to plant the pansies at our cemetery lot in Attalla, I naturally called the mayor there, Charles O'Rear and he found someone right away. It was my good fortune to grow up in Attalla, Alabama at the time I did, and I feel very blessed to have been there. Our children are a daughter, Hartselle, and Scott William Frame, and David Patrick Frame.

Attalla, Alabama My Home (Cherokee)

Henry P. Graham

My earliest recorded relative in this country was John Burnett, who came from England and was with General George Washington at Valley Forge April 3, 1778. John Burnett was the owner of the largest cotton plantation in Virginia and one of his daughters married the governor of North Carolina.

John Burnett's granddaughter, Eliza Burnett, married my great grandfather, Andrew Jackson Sitz who later was wounded at Gettysburg and came home with a musket ball in his shoulder. He came down the Cumberland River and then the Tennessee River in a skiff with a friend, and walked the balance of the way home.

They moved to Attalla and lived in an antebellum home - present location of Brown's Motel. My grandfather, Henry Anderson Sitz, a contractor, was born here and later married Henrietta Moore of Moore's Springs in Little Wills Valley. Jesse Gilliland, who built Gilliland's Covered Bridge, which is now in Pioneer village at Noccalula Falls, married Henry Anderson Sitz's sister. My Mother, Jesse Bena Sitz, married Frances Prentice Graham who came here from Birmingham with my grandparents, George Fenman and Mary Davidson Graham.

The Sitz family came from Germany and settled in the Dutch settlements of Pennsylvania. They later moved to Lincoln County, North Carolina, and in the 1880s to Alabama and settled on Lookout Mountain.

Emily and Anne Graham are active members of the Daughters of the American Revolution (DAR) and United Daughters of Confederacy (UDC).

My grandfather, George Penman Graham, came from Bonneybridge Scotland, arriving in New York Harbor on July 4, 1876, in the middle of the 100th celebration of the Declaration of Independence. Not knowing that all the fireworks was about the celebration, he thought he had arrived in the middle of a war.

He settled in Chicago, where he worked with Thomas Edison in the development of the electric light bulb. He married his childhood sweetheart, Mary Prentice Davidson, who had earlier come over from Scotland with her parents, Frances Prentice and Elizabeth Neal Davidson. These grandparents moved to Birmingham and then Attalla, where my grandfather, who was listed as an engineer in the 1880 census of Cook County, Illinois, helped build Gulf States Steel.

Facts gleaned from the Attalla Library listed on the Internet from a paper by George P. Walker III..

LaFayette visited what is now Attalla in 1825 as a guest of The United States Government. During this time, a French writer, Courter B. Chateaubriand wrote the novel "Attalla, an Indian Maiden."

It was in Attalla that David Brown, an Indian, prepared a "Cherokee Spelling Book."

Attalla was Incorporated on February 5, 1872, with a population of 300, under the name Newton. However, later it was found that there was another town in Alabama named Newton and the name was changed to Attalla in 1893.

Chief Wills, an important Chief of the Cherokee nation, lived in this area and thus the names, Big Wills Valley, Big Wills Creek, Little Wills Valley and Little Wills Creek.

Wills Valley Railroad was the first railroad and was built to run from Chattanooga to Attalla in 1870. This later became Alabama Great Southern railroad (AGS). Attalla was the largest iron ore shipping point in Alabama in the late 1880s and became the railroad center of Northeastern Alabama.

The first hydro electric plant for lighting an entire city was built in Big Wills Valley in 1887 and Attalla had the first electric street lights in the country.

These things I was told - Henry P. Graham

Dr. James H. Wood Sr. had the first automobile in Attalla. It had the large buggy wheels and boys would hold the wheels and the auto did not have enough power to move. Dr. Wood carried a buggy whip to keep the boys from holding the wheels.

The foundation of Dwight Manufacturing Co. was laid in the area of Lake Rhea road. Some of Attalla's founding fathers bought up the property surrounding this Dwight property so Dwight built in Alabama City.

The street car ran from Gadsden to Attalla and turned around at the Attalla Railroad Station. Men who worked at the steel mill and lived in the East side of Attalla would get up when the street-car passed and then catch it on the way back to Alabama City. Street car fare was 5 cents.

Etowah High School was the first senior high school in the area and it was a boarding high school. The students came to school on horses and in buggies and went home on the week-ends. The boys lived on the second floor with the principal and the girls lived with the principal's wife at their home. The first principal's name was Mr. Turnipseed. During this time Etowah won the Southern Junior College football championship.

These things I remember:

My earliest vivid memories are of the old First Baptist church on North Fourth Street and of the large trees and picket fences on Hughes Avenue. We would have to stay in our yard when we had mumps, measles, etc., and could not go near other children. We would just place a toy on the fence and ride away and our friend would ride up to the fence between our yards and get it.

Of course I remember the street cars. Several of my small dogs were killed on the street car tracks and we put nails and pins on the tracks to be pressed by the street car into knives, scissors, etc.

Ed Hamner, Attalla's first attorney, was an authority in Indian and early American history. He had a mercantile store at the corner of Fourth Street and Fourth Avenue. I would sit for hours and visit him as he told me history of this area. There was a blacksmith shop and grist mill across the street from his store.

Mules pulled carts of iron ore from the mines through the downtown area to the Southern Railroad. Tracks went through the area of the present Attalla Post Office. I have been told that there are mine shafts under the present business district of Attalla.

Attalla had a telephone operator that KNEW and TOLD everything. The old Attalla Grammer School on First Street had a fire and the operator plugged in every phone on that side of town and told all subscribers at one time of the fire. Most of the parents beat the fire-truck to the school. If a family needed a doctor at night, the operator could tell them where the doctor was. Yes - Doctors made house calls at this time.

The Ice Man "Mr. Red" was a celebrity during the summer. We would bring out a jar and he would let us pick up the ice chips out of the bottom of his truck. (Of course he had walked on them all morning! Ice was 10 cents for 25 pounds.

The building of the Railroad Underpass provided a multitude of memories. We had to stay back from construction; however, I watched workers from the door of my father's wholesale grocery, The Etowah Grocery Co. I was amazed at the workers throwing red hot bolts from the ground level up to the men on top, who caught them in a small cup.

Lake Rhea was a very popular resort and provided entertainment for young and old most of our lives. People came from counties all around.

During the depression years a large number of men on our street were unemployed and things were tight; however, my father was fortunate enough to stay in the wholesale grocery business.

I went to high school in the old Etowah brick building and graduated in the rock building. The rock building and rock stands of Etowah Bowl were built by the Works Project Administration (WPA) while I was at Etowah. One year we played Emma Samson at homecoming and did not have the money to have a homecoming parade. A recent graduate, who had an airplane, agreed to drop blue and white paper strips on Emma Sansom High School. This was probably not a good idea as it made Sansom so mad they almost beat us.

I had a band during these years. At the last Etowah Golden Age reunion the vocalist of my band sat next to me. I had not seen her since High School

Camp Sibert opened after I left for the South Pacific and was closing when I returned. Soldiers lived with my parents and other families in Attalla during this time. Red Skelton, Mickey Rooney and other movie stars stationed at Camp Sibert, lived at Brown's Motel.

During World War II and the mid 1900s, Attalla was a busy railroad center. It handled approximately 35 trains per day and a large part of the mail and freight for Northeast Alabama arrived and departed from here.

An afternoon of a 5 cent movie at the old Liberty Theatre and two for 1 cent cookies at the Liberty Bakery next door was always enjoyable.

I Remember.....

by Coleman Howard

I was born in Attalla, Alabama on July 5, 1921. The home I was born in was on 5th Avenue. The house was built by Mr. Charlie Waldrop for $1800. Dr. E. K. Hanby delivered me at home as was the custom in those days. The home was later sold to Mr. Dennis McClendon. Everyone has favorite memories that they remember from the past. Some are sad, some are happy and some are clear as yesterday. I remember my Mother gave me a birthday party when I was five years old. Each guest brought a small gift which was customary. I remember Henry Graham wouldn't give me his present and I tried to take it away from him resulting in a spanking on my part.

The white frame school house on First Street where the fire station is located now is where I started my first grade. Our 1st grade teacher was Miss O'Brien and she was nice. Mrs. Elvela Rhea brought Clarence Frost to school that was on our first day. I'm sure we were both a little scared but wouldn't admit it. We survived that first day and after that we made it O.K. That was 75 years ago and Clarence F. and I have remained good friends every since. I consider Henry Jr., his brother, a good friend and ditto for Richard. Henry Jr. was a graduate of the University of Alabama and was to receive a commission in the Navy but unfortunately passed away at a very young 23. Mrs. Rhea fed me many good meals over the years for which I am so grateful.

Later on after the third grade we moved to the brick building which was directly next door. Our 4th grade teacher who was well liked but not as affectionately as Miss O'Brien. I remember we had a lunch room in the basement and for a nickel you could get a cup of soup. I remember there were two boys in our class that were several years older than most of us. One was Edward Byrd and the other was Cotton Taylor and they both delighted in taking our nickels from us. We knew if we reported it the result would be a good beating. Finally I got tired of going hungry from the nickel shortage and challenged Edward to a fight after school. The fight was to take place behind the old Episcopal church across the street from the school. I was scared to death but was afraid to back out so I wouldn't be branded as a coward. Things turned out pretty good for me that day but I was so glad when it was over. They say things have a strange way of working out because Edward Byrd died an alcoholic at an early age. We had classes in the red brick building until the completion of our 8th grade. The Principal and Mrs. French , our home-room teacher in the 8th grade. Mrs. French transferred to Etowah when we entered high school the next year which was fine with me as she was one of my favorite teachers.

One of the most stupid things I ever did , and I did quite a few, was to arrive early on our first day at Etowah. Back then they had what was called "initiation" day. The idea or purpose was to welcome you to Etowah and make you feel at home. Some welcome! I arrived real early that first day thinking they might have pity on me. I was never more wrong. A committee of idiots met me and a few more early arrivals and made us run around the circle in front of the school. Each one would hit us with a belt or paddle, a switch or some object that inflicted pain. That went on for some days - mornings and after classes ended in the afternoon. The pain was pretty severe at times and there was nothing we could do but take it. I felt sorry for Kenneth Riddle as they made him bleed quite a bit. I never initiated anyone the following year since I thought the whole thing was stupid and un-called for.

We entered Etowah during the depression year and most of us were poor. We made up for the hardship by being resourceful in so many ways. We did odd jobs or delivered papers or worked at A & P or Hill's grocery or picked up dry cleaning. Those students who lived in the county and rode busses had plenty of hard work to perform after school. Sometime in the early fall we had a two-week "recess" for cotton picking time. Etowah High meant so much to all of us and we benefited from it every day. I still enjoy my 38 and 39 annuals but its sad to see so many that have passed on. We realized in our senior year that Hitler was just around the corner.

After completion of high school quite a few of us attended college and several went to work at various jobs. I worked at the steel plant and attended Snead Junior College at the same time. After two years at Snead, I was promoted to a much better paying job at the plant. I worked there until I joined the army in early 1943.

Most of the guys I had known and grown up with entered the war in one of the branches of service. We joined because it was our duty and we loved our country. The majority of us served over-seas and I am so very thankful most of us came back intact. I remember "Ma" Childers" gave me a pocket size bible, a gift from the First Baptist Church of Attalla of which I was a member. "Ma Childers" was the most beloved woman in Attalla, always being nice and kind to someone. She and Mr. Childers owned a hotel where they rented rooms and apartments by the week or month. That little Bible was such a comfort in every religious service that we had on Sunday morning regardless of the locale. Each denomination had the use of the tent or shelter we used for one hour. Usually the Jewish service was first, Catholic second and Protestant third. I could hold that small bible in one hand and visualize the First Baptist Church of Attalla having their Sunday morning service. I could plainly see a few of the faithful members, Dr. and Mrs. Hanby, Mr. and Mrs. Spurlock, Dr. Stutts, and always Mr. Dennis and Justin McClendon, the Abercrombie girls, Mr. Eugene Gray, Mr. E. B. Tucker, James Noble and Evelyn Fulgum, Miss Fannie Lou Griffin, Miss Florence Brothers and so many more. I could just see those majestic looking organ pipes that made the music sound so great. I could see "Miss" Mae Killian playing the organ and Mr. Horace Phillips, who was choir director, leading the congregation in song. A few of the choir I remember so vividly—Mrs. E. B. Tucker, Miss Hazel Holland, Mr. and Mrs. Doug Henslee, Marshall Wolf and Pledger Moore. Miss Ola Camp played the piano and filled in for Mrs. Killian on the organ. My thoughts made me remember most of my Sunday School teachers over the many years – Mr. Herbert Camp, Mr. Glen Ward, Mr. Horace Phillips, James Noble Fulgum, La van Garrett, McKinley Gilliland and Mr. E. B. Tucker. I will always be grateful to "Ma Childers" for that small bible she gave me and also to the First Baptist Church of Attalla.

One of my earliest memories of Attalla was an elderly gentleman whose name was Mr. R. Heath. Mr. Heath worked for the Southern Railroad Co., whose job was to help control traffic for the many trains that passed thru Attalla each day. Mr. Heath had two signs he used, one had the Letters "GO" written on both sides and the other sign had the letters "STOP" written on both sides. When a train approached, sometimes a freight and sometimes a passenger train, Mr. Heath would hold up the "STOP" sign and after the train passed he would hold up the "GO" sign. He would then retreat to his small 6' by 6' hut which was big enough for one chair and a pot-bellied stove. Mr. Heath worked for the railroad until the underpass caused his job to be eliminated. The underpass took such a long time to complete and one of the many problems was the underground springs. The springs kept them busy, pumping out water continuously. To this day they still have the same problem as the water seeps through the asphalt causing constant patching. Those two underpasses affected so many people that lived in that area.

After the war several of us went back to school courtesy of Uncle Sam. I went back a couple of years myself and got paid for going since I received a small pension. In the meantime I married a Guntersville girl, Lydle Virginia Powell, and still remain married to the same smart girl. We had two kids, a boy named Robert and a girl named Jane. I'm so proud that they both graduated from Etowah.

Jane graduated from Jacksonville State and also the University of Alabama in Tuscaloosa. Robert graduated from Jacksonville State. Jane was a majorette in the 10th, 11th, and 12th grades at Etowah. Robert played and lettered in basketball, baseball and football at Etowah. We had three grandsons who graduated from college and a grand daughter who graduated from Auburn.

Before entering the armed service I had worked at the steel plant as a staff chemist. It was routine work and several of the older chemists helped me adjust after being promoted from a chemist helper. The pay was good at that time but the hours were terrible. One week I worked days, the next I would work all night. The different shifts kept your system confused all the time. Mr. John Middleton was my boss and he promised to hold my job for six months from the time of my discharge from the army. I knew his word was good and he would keep his promise. The truth of the matter is I didn't want to go back to those hours and kept making excuses to myself. One day by chance S. W. Kelly introduced me to John Rosick who was starting up a new Produce Co. He offered me a job as a salesman on a generous salary plus a commission over a specified amount in sales. I worked for John the entire length of time he stayed in business.

After a year he decided to call it quits and later went into the construction business. I decided to try my luck in the produce business as I had some real good paying customers I didn't want to lose. Attalla Pipe lunch room, Attalla City Schools, F. R. Sims, Gadsden High lunch room, J. E. Smith grocery—just to mention a few. John let me have one of his big trucks on credit and gave me a year to pay for it. I had a small truck so I was on my way. Things worked out O.K. and I paid the truck off on time. I stayed in business for forty one years and left never owing anyone a dime. The secret of being successful in produce business is doing your own buying and having a good relationship with your buyer. Another important thing is to pay your bills promptly and give good dependable service. The much larger chain stores eventually closed the small neighborhood stores as there was no way they could compete. I was sixty seven when I called it a day and grateful that I lasted that long.

Although so many of us don't live in Attalla, we still consider Attalla our home. We still shop every week in Attalla and go to church in Attalla every Sunday. We plan to be interred in the Attalla Cemetery, Oak Hill, among our friends and relatives. I'm proud to have been born in Attalla and proud to call Attalla my home. Sincerely, Coleman Howard.....

My History of Attalla, Alabama

---Gordon Roswell Isbell, Jr.

Gordon R. Isbell, Jr. was born April 12, 1923. Parents Mr. and Mrs. Gordon Roswell Isbell, Sr. Born on Christopher Street Gadsden, Alabama, moved to Attalla in 1923 where Gordon R. Isbell Sr. ran Isbell and Hallmark Furniture Co. on 4th Street Attalla next to Merchants and Farmers Bank that Mr. C. R. Shepherd was President. I remember my Mama and Daddy taking me to Sunday School at First Methodist Church of Attalla. We lived at 712 4th Street in Mrs. Pettit's House, who lived next door. Their daughter married Mr. Thompson, head of Gulf State Steel. After he died Mrs. Ruth Pettit Thompson married Mr.R. B. Kyle whose homeplace was where the parking lot of the present Etowah County Courthouse on right side is today. Mr. Kyle owned the whole block where Pollock Automobile is today.

I used to go next door when I was a small boy and take my quart of milk and Mrs. Pettit's pint of milk back to Mama and Daddy's house because I liked the small pint bottle better. Next door Mrs. Gray lived in a big 2-story home. She had a boarding house and she served many meals. Her daughter was Mrs. Freda Ray and her sister was Nell Jo Ray whose husband was Rip Reagan. He was a Veterinarian then and had a hardware store in Attalla where Frank Ledbetter Hardware was later. Then football coach at Emma Sansom High School in Alabama City, later principal –Colonel in Army World War II. Mrs. Nell Jo worked at Alabama City Bank, Mr. James Little (what a great friend he was to me when I opened a furniture store in Alabama City in 1949 across from Marvin's Hardware.) Dear Friend of 55 years Alan Cohn. When Colonel Reagan got out of the service, he ran for probate judge of Etowah County, which office he held until he died. While living as a small boy at 712 4th Street we had wide steps up to our house and had concrete slab bannisters. Fourth street was paved by convicts who started work at 6:00 am. My Mama , Mrs. Gordon R. Isbell, Sr. made punch and tea-cake cookies and I would take them to the convicts and they really appreciated mama making punch and cookies for them. Captain Able was in charge of the convicts and one morning daddy hollered at my mama that there were convicts all around our house. They were putting out shrubbery around the house and cleaning the yard because my mama had been so nice. She made them cookies or cakes two to three times a week. One Christmas morning a convict came up and knocked on our front door—all the others were in the yard with Capt. Able. They sang Merry Christmas and brought me a little metal truck. It just proved to me as a small little boy, if you will be nice to people, they will try to be nice to you.

In 1929 I was 6 years old and Rev. John Rice came to First Methodist Church as our pastor. I remember his son, John. My Mama, Mrs. Gordon R. Isbell, Sr was president of the WMS, the average attendance of Sunday School averaged 280. My Uncle, Reverend William Harris was elected district superintendent of our district. In 1931 Mrs. C. R. Shepherd was elected delegate to the annual conference - Uncle Bill Harris returned as president elder, he married my mama's sister Aunt Margaret and they had 2 daughters, Margaret and Susie, and 2 sons Dr. Bill and John Harris. John, my first cousin, talked the least. Once a week he walks 5 to 10 miles at 4:00 am at mall at Hoover that my friends Bill and John Harbert built.

Mrs. C. R. Shepherd gave the chimes in our tower at First Methodist Church of Attalla that our city of Attalla has enjoyed all these years. Mrs. C. R. Shepherd gave the chimes in honor of Mr. C. R. Shepherd. She was such a lovely person. They were the richest family of Attalla, it was always said. In 1941 I was president of the student body of Etowah High School. Mama taught English and Latin; Mama used to ask each student she taught to pray to God at each meal and thank God for their meal. Each night to get on their knees and pray- "Lay me down to sleep"...Plus thank God for their mama and daddy, and their sisters and brothers and their friends. Then go to Sunday School and church each Sunday of their choice and ask their parents to go with them. My parents, Mr. and Mrs. Gordon R. Isbell, Sr. won many people's souls for Christ. Hardly a week goes by that someone stops by our store, Isbell and Hallmark Furniture Store. We have been in west Gadsden since 1906. Some say my mama and my daddy saved their souls and their families for Christ. My daddy was treasurer of First Methodist Church Attalla for 52 years. He started the Upper Room Sunday School class and taught for 57 years. My sister, Annette Isbell Hornsby - God let her catch polio. This is 2004 and she has not walked in 63 years. I have told so many people the past 63 years - stop fussing because you can walk and my sister cannot. I have never heard her fuss except when Auburn Beat Alabama in football!

When mama and daddy took Annette to see Sister Kenny at Sheltering Arms Hospital in Minneapolis, Minnesota at 13 years of age and Mrs. C. R. Shepherd had to go because she loved our family, our world would be so much better if all of us could be better Christians like my parents and Mrs. C. R. Shepherd. Mrs. C. R. Shepherd lived across the street from my parents. Mr. Shepherd was president of Merchant and Farmers Bank. One morning he came out of his house to get in his two door car and it would not back up so he called Mr. Ralph Brown Service Station to come to his house to see if they could fix his car. Mr. Ralph Brown came up at once. He told Mr. Shepherd that someone had jacked up his car and stolen his four wheels.

Mr. Ralph Brown had a motel behind his Texaco service station and he was the brother of Mrs. Clarence Jones. Mr. Brown's wife, Mrs. Kate Brown with Mrs. Clarence Jones, Mrs. Horace Banks and my mama, Mrs. Gordon R. Isbell, Sr. ran the Sunday School Department at First Methodist Church of Attalla. We had an all time high of 335 people that were in attendance. First Methodist Church of Attalla sure wish that we had that many now in 2004. Rev. B. F. Tingle came to First Methodist Church of Attalla in 1932. What a great pastor! Great family two sons two daughters, one of whom was Polly, was in high school and I was in grammar school but I remember how pretty she was and how nice she was. Goes back to say that it doesn't cost anything to be sweet and nice to everybody.

In 1934 Rev. W. Dubose was our pastor - great person and great family. Our church really enjoyed him and his family. In 1937 Rev. Marvin Heflin was our pastor and his son, Howell, went to Etowah with Martha Lou Jones Riddle, Henry Rhea, and Clarence Frost Rhea and all 4 of them went to college at the University of Alabama. Howell went to Birmingham College, first law school in Alabama and later Judge in Montgomery and later U. S. Senator.

The present chandelier in the sanctuary of the First Methodist Church was first owned by the J. R. Brown family. For some reason the chandelier was later discovered in the back of the O. K. Barbershop when May Cole and Freda Ray found it. Then it was moved to the sanctuary of the Church and there it gleams today.

Martha Lou Jones (now Riddle) was the first girl to be president of Etowah County High School. Later my sister (Mrs. Cain (Kathryn Isbell) O'Rear, was second girl to be president of Etowah County student body.

Mrs. Sep Scales lived on 3rd street of Attalla. Every Monday she came and picked up our dirty clothes to clean. I love Aunt Sep Scales. I used to deliver her paper, The Birmingham News, and when I got engaged to my lovely wife, Iris Taylor Johnson of Jasper , Alabama, in 1952 and married her on February 14, 1953, I took her to meet Aunt Sep Scales as most people called her. She said, Mr. Gordon Isbell, you sho found you a beautiful lady. I said thank you, Aunt Sep, but when did you start calling me, Mr. Isbell? You have always called me Gordy. I never want you to ever call me anything but Gordy. She gave us a cup of tea and cake. Iris and I visited Aunt Sep Scale very often and brought our sons to see Aunt Sep as they were born. Our son Dr. Gordon R. Isbell III remembers Aunt Sep Scales, my other sons, Hal and Gil, were too small to remember. I cherish the memories of Aunt Sep Scales.

Eugene Worthy on 15th street was another of my growing up friends: he could really draw. I still have a picture he drew of Santa Claus and his sled and reindeer. We use to fish on Little Wills creek behind Dr. and Mrs. Rip Reagan. We would pick sweet shrubs on the creek bank and put it in a small cloth tobacco bag and sell them at Walker Drug Store for a dime. Why did women buy? The sweet shrubs made them smell good. Another great person I knew was Mrs. Lola Mae Lipscomb Hayes who lived on First Street in Attalla. Her husband, Isaiah Hayes, worked at Attalla Pipe Shop in 1920. He bought his furniture from my daddy at Isbell and Hallmark Furniture in 1920 after he married Lola Mae Lipscomb in May 1920. They bought furniture from our store for 83 years. I remember when I was 12 years old, I would go with my daddy every Saturday to collect. Many Saturdays Mrs. Oscar Lee (Lola Mae) Hayes would have me a cup of hot chocolate and 3 marshmallows. I called her on her birthday for 55 years.

Another great Attalla family, Mr. O'Rear started a furniture store in late 1900, then son Mr. Bud O"Rear took over and his son, Conley, now runs O'Rear Furniture in Attalla. They are the oldest furniture store in Etowah County. My company, Isbell and Hallmark Furniture Store is the second oldest in Etowah County but we are the oldest in Gadsden and to my knowledge, oldest Retailer in Gadsden. Also Charles O'Rear, who is Attalla's Mayor goes to the same church as I do.

Another great family in Attalla, Dr. C. B. Forman that lived across the street from First Methodist Church in Attalla. He started First National Bank in Attalla and a factory on north Third Street in Attalla. I had the honor to be on First National Bank of Attalla's Board for 12 years. When I moved to Gadsden I was honored to be on Central Bank of the South Board for 13 years - my son, Dr. Gordon R. Isbell III, took my place for the past 18 years.

Not bragging but to let people know how fortunate I was to be raised in Attalla and knowing so many wonderful people who so kindly helped me to learn in each phase of my wonderful life. First I thank God, second I thank my wonderful Mama and Daddy - Mr. and Mrs. Gordon R. Isbell, Sr. and third to so many people that really took an interest in me and really helped me and were so nice to me these 81 years, April 12, 2004. At 8 years old I delivered Birmingham newspaper. I worked for my dear friend, Clarence Rhea. Clarence made $1.15 a week. He paid me 15 cents a week. I tell him today he still owes me some money cause I did the work - kidding - Later got my own paper route. I was making $1.14 a week. My daddy asked me how much was I giving to God each week. I said 10 cents Daddy. My daddy taught me another good lesson of life. Daddy said you must give God 10% net

on the net income. So I started giving God 12 cents a week.
Daddy always said to do this the rest of your life and God will
always take care of you. I feel God has always given me more
than I deserve…a great Mama and Daddy, two great sisters,
a lovely wonderful wife, Iris that I love so much. February
14, 2004 we have been married 51 years. God blessed Iris
and me with 3 great sons Dr. Gorden Isbell III, a local dentist,
my son, Hal, and my son, Gil Isbell, a lovely daughter in law,
Leigh Hillyer Isbell (Hal's wife) and son Gilmer Frank Isbell,
who runs my store, Isbell and Hallmark Furniture, 80 years in
West Gadsden. Then God gave us grandchildren 3 to Gordon
III and 3 to Hal. What a joy they have been.

I was selling Birmingham News 5 cents on Saturday and
10 cents on Sunday. I was at Attalla Railroad Station one
Saturday and I went up to this train car and FBI would not let
me on. He said sorry you can't get on this train—President
Roosevelt is on his way to Jasper, Alabama to Senator
Bankhead's funeral. I went to Train engine I, sold them a
paper each week. I went down to President Roosevelt's car.
The FBI man said I thought I told you that you couldn't see
President Roosevelt. I saw President Roosevelt. I said my
Mama and Daddy voted for President Roosevelt. I am an
American. The president said come on in, Son, he said to
have a seat. Who are you? I said Sir, I am Gordon R. Isbell,
Jr., he said how much are your papers. I said "5 cents, sir. He
gave me 25 cents and said when you are in Washington come
to see me. If I had kept this 25 cents I believe it would really
be worth something or at least good for a great conversation.

Next I went to work on Saturday for A & P food store next
to Walker Drug Store 6:00 am to 12 pm for $3.00—probably
more than I was worth. But I learned so much. Some lady
came in and said, Gordy, give me a poke, please. I went to
Mr. Gus the Manager, he sent me to Mr. Cooper, head of the
meat market, he sent me to Shorty Rakstraw in back and he
said "Gordy a poke is a paper sack! We both laughed. My

next job was at Stewart Drug Store, 7ᵗʰ through 12ᵗʰ grade. Mr. Leon Locklear "The greatest man I ever knew except my lovely Great Daddy. Mr. Locklear taught me so much. He let me make mistakes, always correcting me in such a nice way. I loved Mr. Locklear and his family. I thought I was a great soda jerker. Many Sundays we would have 2 to 6 people catching curb from Walker Drugstore to Lowi's department store at the other end of the block. I realize how lucky I was. Gosh, I fixed so many sodas, ice cream cones, milkshakes, people would come up to me and say "You are the best soda jerker ever! May not be true But I am so glad I remember the good times in my life.

Mr. Leon Locklear's wife, Ruby, whose father, Mr. Nabors, was a Methodist minister. Her sister, Mrs. Opal Lee (used to be tax collector for Etowah County), Mrs. Frances, her sister, sang in the choir at First Methodist Church. Mr. Locklear took me to 1ˢᵗ out of town football game in Gadsden vs. Bessemer Thanksgiving day, then that afternoon Alabama and Georgia. I believe Georgia won. Then to Rev. and Mrs. Nabors for Thanksgiving dinner. Mrs. Ruby Locklear's brother, James Nabor's family was there, he worked for McKesson and Robins, drug wholesale chain. When I was six years old one morning at breakfast my Daddy asked if I took any money out of his watch pocket in his coat. I said yes sir, daddy said, how much and I said 2 dimes and a nickel. He said a quarter - what was I going to do with it. I said going to Walker Drug Store, get a 10 cent yo-yo. What would I do with the 15 cent balance—going to Stewart Drug Store and buying 10 cent yo-yo. What difference between Walker Drug yo-yo. It sings! What are you doing with 5 cent balance. I'm going to Mr. Condray's, next to First National Bank, owned by Dr. Forman, and get a 36"piece of red licorice for 5 cents. Recently on going to Birmingham, we stopped in Trussville and I bought a 36" piece of red licorice, now $1.25.

My Daddy, Gordon R. Isbell, Sr., said if you ever need money or anything come to your mama or me and we will get it for you if we can. I never forgot that as long as Mama and Daddy lived. Only once daddy said he was not in a position to. Will tell you my junior year in High school.

Went to grammar school on First Street in Attalla—First grade, Mrs. Gaines, Second Grade, Mrs. Herbert Camp (Mr. Camp worked for Post Office), third grade, Mrs. Jewel Tucker, her sister, Mrs. Herbert Camp. Second grade we went to window to see Mrs. Clarence Jones' uncle - (Mr. Nicholson, who had a bottle company - Orange Crush- in Argentina, South America.) The person who was the governor of Argentina picked Mr. Nicholson out. Later he opened a branch business in Cuba and Katherine Cole Frame, Martha Lou Jones Riddle, and her friend, Florence Gaskin Cole of Birmingham, visited Mr. Nicholson there in March 1947. (I'm told that the four girls had a taxi driver take them to the race track and help them with their bets.) But back to the second grade. Brad Nicholson, while visiting in Attalla, was in our second grade and Mrs. Camp let us go to the window to see Brad go to New York with his mama and two brothers to catch a boat to Argentina and to return to their home there. I was in Atlanta two months ago on August 23, 2003 to celebrate Brad's 80th birthday with his wife, Elsa, and his daughter, Sharman. Sorry you missed it! The spread for 40 of Brad's friends was catered by his daughter, Sharman.

In the Fourth Grade, Miss Willie Griffin had a picture of her Dad's picture studio which was next to the Ralph Brown Texaco Service Station - Miss Griffin taught us to never eat the dough on the inside of biscuits. My Mama thought that was horrible. The Fifth and Sixth grade teacher was Mrs. E. G. Pilcher. Her husband was a lawyer and her daughter was Mary. Mrs. Pilcher was probably the best teacher I ever had. She kept me after school 2 to 3 days a week trying to teach me my ings. Plus Mrs. E. G. Pilcher taught me so much. She took an interest in me and she was a teacher so much like my Mama, Mrs. Gordon R. Isbell, Sr. She thought it was her duty to teach students to learn that they should grow up and be something and do something good. To go to High School and Go to College - be somebody and act like a Christian should. I will always love Mrs. E. G. Pilcher for not only what she did for me, Gordon R. Isbell, Jr. but what she did for all her students. We have many great teachers, thank God, but those who know they are not doing their best should follow Mrs. E. G. Pilcher and Mrs. Gordon R. Isbell, Sr. Thank God for all they did.

My Seventh Grade Teacher married Pedro Black, the football Coach at Etowah High School. (There was a Junior High division for children who rode the busses, grades 6,7,8 and Senior High for students from Attalla, grades 9,10,11,12. (Etowah County High School was the first high school in Etowah County.) Mr. Carl Baxter came to be principal of Etowah High School 1938, 1939, 1940. He had school clean inside and out, bathrooms shined for the first time and if you wrote on the wall or bathroom, Mr. Baxter was the best detective in the world. He found who did! Their parents had to come to school, had to pay and their child had to clean and paint. They were spanked 2nd time, 3rd time expelled. Mr. Baxter was the greatest principal I ever saw. Mrs. Gordon R. Isbell, Sr., my Mama, came to Etowah High School from Gaston High School where she taught from 1933 to 1937. My Mama taught English and Latin. We had many great teachers my four years at Etowah High School.

I had many many honors that my classmates helped me to earn -Beta Club - Senior Council. In 1940, my Junior year, I was honored to be elected as Junior Class President. Mr. Carl Baxter decided to let us have a junior prom if I sold enough tickets to pay for the bill. I sold $375 in tickets to hire a band from Birmingham-Southern College. We had policemen, parents students. No alcohol beverages, no beer, no smoking and no hanky panky. Biggest crowd ever! Junior and Senior classes decorated, students assigned to dance with each teacher at least twice. This was a tie, evening dress or Sunday go dress up if evening dress not available. Refreshments served. Duties were assigned that everything went as it should. Gordon R. Isbell, Jr. brought each person to be recognized who helped plan this event. Each teacher brought to front then Mr. Carl Q. Baxter, our Principal—an award was given to him for allowing our Junior Class to have this affair. Student assigned to each teacher. Gordon R. Isbell, Jr. asked Mr. and Mrs. Baxter to start, then each teacher and assigned student to the teacher was introduced. Students went wild, then special dance for 11th Grade class. Someone was assigned to each girl and boy and Gordon announced each person. The orchestra leader from Birmingham-Southern honored Gordon's date, Jane Banks, by dancing with her. Then Gordon and Jane did a half jitter bug dance. The orchestra was really accepted. They played two extra pieces. "Stardust" , Gordon requested. This was a night all present remember. Each student's parents were invited and urged to come - many of them danced a special slow piece. After expenses, we made over $300.00 profit which went to the school from the junior class.

George Barnett and Gordon R. Isbell, Jr. ran for president of student body. Gordon organized a big committee of two students on each bus, two to four students for 7th through 12th grade classes. Hand written cards given to each student on bus and each class. Signs all over hall and each bus for weeks. Gordon had soft drink bottle top he had gotten from both drug stores, all grocery stores. Anybody sold soft drink, cork taken out, vote Isbell, tape put on bottle cap. Signs said "He is short, he is swatchy, Isbell for President of Student Body." Signs in hall and buses "Farmers Friend Vote Isbell for President of Student Body." George Barnett had his sister and friends make flower and sign like a poppy, saying "Barnett for President Body."

Last two weeks Gordon had signs from top of buildings hanging down saying "vote for Isbell for Student Body as so the farmers friend. <u>The Gadsden Times</u> even came over and put on front page, <u>The Attalla Weekly</u> had George and Gordon picture and signs. Gordon had signs in Stewart Drug Store, Attalla Cleaners and A & P where Gordon worked. George had sign in Hill's grocery store where he worked. Both banks would not let them put a sign in the banks. George and Gordon and all their helpers had a great time doing this. They were the best of friends all their lives.

Gordon and Jimmy Wood started a dance hall called Wood and Isbell Dance Hall. Every Friday after a football game to 12:00 pm students (only 15 cents single and 25 cents a couple. Cold drinks 5 cents cokes, Dr. Pepper, RC (belly wash) no smoking, no alcohol allowed - only high school students, music of best bands in land by record. You must act like a lady or gentleman or you will be asked to leave. Parents were invited 20 cents per couple. Have good clean fun! This went on Junior and Senior year during football season. Jimmie and Gordon made some money, gave young place to meet, fun was had by all.

Chief of Police Glen Brown, Policemen Mr. Keener and Mr. Fowler saw that order was had. Alabama Department of Revenue came to see Jimmie Wood and Gordon R. Isbell, Jr. to see why they did not have a license. Met at city hall building next door- Mayor Charles Wood Burke came to the rescue of Jimmie Wood and Gordon Isbell, Jr. by saying they were making a place for school kids to go after football games and keep kids off street, church endorsed. Mayor Charles Wood Burke even came several times with Mrs. Burke. Jimmie Wood's and Gordon R. Isbell Jr. parents came several times also.

Homer Turner Jr. took up the money and helped change the records. Homer graduated from Auburn University, later one of Alabama Power Co. Vice Presidents. Gordon got Homer in Sigma Nu Fraternity as Mr. Turner did Gordon. James B. McElroy graduated from University of Alabama, played in orchestra at university. Gordon got James B. McElroy in Sigma Nu fraternity, later James B. McElroy came back to Etowah County as Dr. James B. McElroy. He was a great internal medicine doctor. Jimmie and Gordon used to kid Homer and James that they helped them to be famous.

Cowboys of Attalla with their ponies: Martha Lou Jones Riddle, daughter of Mr. and Mrs. Clarence Jones, 5th Avenue - Santa brought her a pony called Prince. Dot Tarpley Holmes, daughter of Mr. and Mrs. A. P. Tarpley , 5th street Attalla had Santa bring Dot a pony called Nancy. Mrs. A. P. Tarpley, Dot's Mother, was a florist. She had a florist in Gadsden next to the Printup Hotel and later moved her shop down the street from the Reich Hotel. Katherine Cole Frame, daughter of Mr. and Mrs. Bill Cole, 5th Ave. Attalla had Santa bring Katherine a pony called Dixie. Mr. Cole had financial and furniture business in Gadsden.

The three girls became so famous with their ponies, Gordon R. Isbell, Jr., son of Mr. and Mrs. Gordon R. Isbell Sr. 5th Street wrote Santa for a pony. Christmas morning Gordon Jr. goes in living room by Christmas tree, there was a cowboy hat, shirt, pants, boots, box cherry candy (29 cents a box) tangerine, apple, orange, a cap pistol. Gordon Jr. started crying "Where is my pony". His Mama and Daddy with two sisters, Annette and Kathryn went to front porch: there was a buddy saddle blanket, whip, brace - No pony. Buster Tarpley, Dot Tarpley"s brother, who lived down the street, got in car with Mr. Gordon R. Isbell Sr., took right turn at Gaston High School, went to Murray"s Crossing to Uncle Charley Miller's home where they got the pony for Gordon R. Isbell, Jr. Brought him to 712 5th Street, Attalla. Gordon Jr. called him, Dixie and he was a happy little boy.

Martha Lou Jones, Dot Tarpley, Katherine Cole and their little boy-friend, Gordon R. Isbell, Jr. had so much fun. They rode all over town in the City of Attalla parade and school functions. The kids in Attalla really enjoyed these four ponies. They brought much pleasure and happiness to this great community of Attalla. Martha Lou, Dot, Katherine and Gordon R. Isbell, Jr. even let little kids and disabled, all races, ride their ponies free to help those that didn't have a pony to have some enjoyment in life. They got more out of this than those that enjoyed the ride. It taught us it is better to give than to receive and that is the golden rule.

On Saturday's Mr. Jack Brown, the Manager of Liberty Theater in Attalla would let Gordon R. Isbell, Jr, his pony, Dixie, his buggy and Shenny Worthy put signs about movie being shown at Liberty Theater in Attalla. Gordon R. Isbell, Jr. and Shenny would go all over town for 5 cents. Kids could ride 2 blocks and get the thrill of their lives. Gordon Jr. even had a 1 cent sucker as a bonus for them. Gordon Jr. and Sheeny got free passes to the picture show. They had to sit upstairs. Godron Jr. would go to A & P and get 2 black cow suckers and split a Powerhouse for 10 cents, split a belly washer (R. C. Cola) WOW they had a lot of fun. Gordon Jr. still talks about the great days of his boyhood in Attalla. Gordon Jr. often says the people were so good to him and helped him to have a better tomorrow.

Gordon R. Isbell, Jr. graduated from Etowah High School on May 28, 1941. He started to Auburn University June 1, 1941. Now Gordon said this is one of the many mistakes he has made in his life. He says to young people don't rush life, it will come. Take it easy. Study hard. Work hard, and take time to smell the roses along life's way. He said he wished he hadn't wanted to rush but take one step at a time, he wished he had traveled more, cause when God lets you find and gives you a lovely wife as he did in letting him have as his wife, Iris Taylor Johnson Isbell. He says 51 years with Iris has been so great, then God gave Iris and Gordon 3 great boys. Dr. Gordon R. Isbell III, a dentist in Gadsden, son Hal in Birmingham, son Gil who is manager of Isbell and Hallmark Furniture where they have been in business for over 98 years. Leigh, Hal's wife is a great daughter in law. We have 6 wonderful grandchildren. Gordon says God has been so good these 80 plus years. Gordon R. Isbell, Jr. is so grateful that so many people, his Mama and Daddy and God and his Son, Jesus Christ has helped to accomplish so much in his 80 plus years. There are so many great, lovely people that have meant so much to the Gordon R. Isbell, Sr. and Junior's family and others have had the honor to live in Attalla. Just a few in Attalla, my parents, Mr. and Mrs. Gordon R. Isbell, Sr. 712 5th street. Next door, Homer Burke, my dear friend who helped me build my first tree house, his Mama and Daddy, where I spent so many days. Sister Frannie later lived in Texas, other sister lived in Alexander City. The house behind Mama and Daddy, Stanley Holcomb-great parents. Stanley married my dear friend all through school the lovely Inez Waters on Stowers Hill South 3rd Street. Beautiful daughter. Across the street 713 5th Street Mr. and Mrs. Ward. He was with Walworth Co (Attalla Pipe Shop), son Bill in Anniston, Beautiful daughter Gail married Rip Reagan, great conductor of Emma Sansom, now director of music Gadsden State. Son Rip, Jr., director of Gadsden High Band. Saw Gail Feb.21,2004 Gadsden Kiwanis Pancake Day, over 8,000 came. Gail in blue outfit, I said "Should of had white belt, let people know you were Attallian (That means raised Attalla and went to Etowah High School.) Next door to Ward's 711 5th Street Eric Grimsley use to be head of Attalla Pipe Shop. He was so good to all of us kids, often took us to Charlotte Story's Mama and Daddy's grocery, left of First Methodist Church of Attalla, buy us a Buffalo Rock drink and 2 banana kisses 2 for 5 cents. Next Mr. and Mrs. Dick and Evelyn Dupre, daughter, Allison, in Florida, brother Bob in Huntsville. Much younger than my Mama and Daddy but often had them to their parties with Jim and Lyda Wood, Rip and Nell Joe Reagan, Ril and Undine Williams. Mrs. Undine's parents, Mr. and Mrs. Case owned most property where Camp Siberton was. He let Jimmie Wood and us use his paddle boat and fish. He let us cut his cattails on Saturday, ride our bikes to Walker Drug Store and sold them for 5 cents each. Mr. Dick Dupre's Daddy, Oscar DuPre owned Attalla Funeral Home next door to A & P, two doors down from Walker Drug. Also next door was Dupre Hardware. His brother, Charles (a great golfer, sister Carolyn married fine person, Donald Porch. He came to my furniture store in Alabama City, Gordon R. Isbell, Jr. Home Furnishing and told me he was moving to Tuscaloosa. He wanted me to have his 1 share in Gadsden Country Club for $150.00. Sure glad he did. I have really enjoyed playing golf there for 55 years; a share would cost much more today. In 1941 when my oldest sister, Annette, caught Polio, the Dupre's were there each day along with Mrs. C. R. Shepherd. The Dupres and Mrs. Shepherd were just what God wanted all of us to be. We will never forget their love and concern.

Mr. T. C. Banks built a big big house on the lot next to my Mama and Daddy. Next Mr. Guest had a fine son, Seaborn, who lived in the next house. Miss Ida Cox married Mr. Lamar Smith, who was a banker in Gadsden, when he died Miss Ida married Dr. Slaton, a Methodist. Minister. Dot Tarpley lived across the street, her Mama, Ruby Tarpley, had a florist in her house. Son Buster had a car lot across from Isbell and Hallmark Furniture. Dot married Roger Holmes, who lived on Hughes Avenue. He used to work at Stewart Drug, then went to Auburn and I think after he served in World War II, he went to work for Babcock and Wilcox in Atlanta.

Evelyn Stevenson lived across the street, brother was a nice fellow and his wife also lived there. I believe Mr. Stevenson worked at Post Office. Next door were Clyde Childers and his wife Helen Childers. Clyde worked at Goodyear, retired and coached Etowah High. Helen taught school, played organ at First Methodist Church in Attalla. Most of my young days Mrs.

93

Easley (Helen's Mother) had a boarding house next to Dr. C. B. Forman's house in Attalla which is now part of Ferguson Florist. Mrs. Easley had a second daughter, Mary Walker.

In 1945 Mrs. Clyde (Helen) Childers was choir director and organist at First Methodist. Wow! Helen was great. Mrs. Clarence Jones (Mae Brown Jones) was President of Woman's Society. Mrs. Mae Brown Jones raised in First Methodist Church of Attalla, one of the greatest women in Attalla. Mrs. Mae practiced and did what my daddy used to say: God put us on this earth to save souls for Christ. If anyone ever did, Mrs. Mae Jones did. Her daughter, Martha Lou Jones, followed right in her Mama's footsteps. She was the first girl to be President of the Junior Class at Etowah. She went to University of Alabama and was a leader as we all expected. She married a fine Auburn graduate from Attalla, Kenneth A. Riddle. He and his Mama lived on 5th Avenue. Martha Lou and Kenneth had 3 sons. I see Mrs. Mae in Martha Lou running things. Martha Lou Jones Riddle has gotten up this history of Attalla but original idea came from Katherine Cole Frame. She has gotten so many of us that grew up in Attalla to take part. She called me the other day, ready to go to press, need your input now! I told her as soon as I could, I still have Isbell and Hallmark Furniture to run plus lots of coals in fire. When you see Martha Lou Jones Riddle, thank her for pushing all of us and like her Mama, Martha Lou is great. She should have been an Army General. She would be one of the best America could ever have.

In 1945 Rev. A. Tillman and his spouse, Ann, came as our pastor at First Methodist. What a hit he made! He wore a collar like he was an Episcopalian minister. Our members loved it and we all loved his wife, Ann, also. He later came back as district superintendent and he and his wife represented God in the best way. I talked with him last week-March 2004-, his health is bad but is still Perrie Tillman. In 1950 Gordon R. Isbell, Jr., Secretary, Gordon R. Isbell, Sr. Treasurer.

94

Rev. Hershel Hammer, Pastor-he and his wife just great big baseball fans. Hershel, one of the best. In my 80 years and oldest member of First Methodist, I loved all ministers except 2, ain't bad is it?

Clarence F. Rhea Vice-Chairman -43 years great service he and his family have made to our church. His great wife, Marie, and they have a daughter, Dr. Elvela Rhea, a dentist, her husband is also a dentist. Sons, Judge Bill Rhea, wife Teresa, their children are Laney, Hal, Donald, Joy, Preston and Holly. Richard and wife Debra, children Rebecca, Drew, Kacie and Katie Watford. Where is Donald? Wow! 16 Rheas, sure can't let one be on payroll if fired one would lose 16 members at once. Don't know if anyone has served God more than the Rheas have.

Gordon R. Isbell, Jr. put in a new system for Sunday School. Each teacher taught every other Sunday. The reason is because they had two weeks to prepare and the second reason is it gave twice the number of teachers. This meant better attendance at school and church. Gordon, Jr. got Olive McDonald and her sister, Virginia, to take over the youth group. The two had parties at their home at least once a month on the Boaz Highway. They served lots of hot dogs, hamburgers, punch, plenty of soft drinks, ice cream, candy and games. The youth department really grew. Olive McDonald had an Insurance Co., also handled Bell South Telephone. When we built new parsonage I asked her to put a telephone in each room. Olive McDonald gladly did and she paid for it.

Mr. and Mrs. J. A. Todd came to Attalla and started Attalla Compress Buckle Co. on North 3rd Street. They had 2 great sons, L. B. Todd married Gaynell Killian. They had two wonderful daughters, Donna Todd Vance married Harry and had two great sons, Wes is a golfer in Atlanta and works at Sun Trust Bank. Cliff is a doctor and going to study to be a heart doctor. L. B. and Gaynell did so much for First Methodist

Church. Brother Byron Todd died at 37 years old. He and his wife, Nena, had two sons, Charles, deceased, and Jim Todd married Margaret Ann Weaver. When her Mama Marquite died, she lived with my Mama and Daddy. Byron Todd had a bus pick up 40 to 50 kids each Sunday, feed them and if they needed clothes or other things. Byron got it for them and brought them to First Methodist Church of Attalla. If each of us did this all of our churches would be full. During World War II, Byron rented the rear of Mr. Clarence Jones' building and made some war materials. Also in Attalla he had a bowling alley, jewelry store, newsstand, owned Gadsden baseball club. I say Byron was a Christian first, shared with others, successful businessman—we need more like Byron Todd.

Mr. and Mrs. Edgar Lee-Mr. Edgar worked at First National Bank of Attalla, (President Dr. C. B. Forman - refer to article by Mary Ellen Luttrell Stewart) - and sang in First Methodist Choir for years +++. He was a great leader. Son Robert Lee and Wife, fabulous Opal Lee, Tax Collector Etowah County, other daughter Mary Frances Lee Farley married to Alex Farley, cotton broker. Great Attallians. Other sister, Ruby, married Leon Locklear, 2nd Daddy to Gordon Isbell,Jr.... owned Stewart Drug Store with Mr. Smith. What a Christian fine man he was. God honored me to let me know him.

In 1968 Foster Talley, Board Chairman, married to Katherine Walker. Dr. and Mrs. Sid Christian invited church to their son's place, Dr. John in Scottsboro. We sure had a great time. 1970 Dewey Stansell, Board Chairman. What a great job he did! Dewey managed his daddy in law's Southern Hardware. What a great voice in the choir at First Methodist Church! Sure miss Dewey and his wife, Billie Ruth. Harold Walker, Vice President of Board

January 3, 1971, a sad sad day in the lives of all at First Methodist Church of Attalla. Dr. Sid Christian went to live with God. Once Sid Christian said he wanted to see our sanctuary filled while he was our pastor. It was at his funeral. How great Dr. Sid and his wife, Polly Christian were.

In 1971 Gordon R. Isbell, Jr. was at a Methodist Church conference, coming down steps from a balcony a beautiful 27 year old lady. Gordon stepped up one step and kissed her on her cheek. She said "who are you?" Our new great Minister Bill Bostick from Tuscaloosa said he is Gordon R. Isbell, Jr., your new financial chairman. Bill and Judy Bostick made a hit like no one ever had. Young for one thing. I have visited with them at least once a month, never missed their birthdays or anniversary. He did my Mama and Daddy's funerals. He will do mine if he is living in 2024. I hope to be 105 years old and pray I make it with good mind and health.

In 1971 Rev. Bill and Judy Bostick returned heritage Sunday. Rev. Tillman and his lovely wife, Ann, preached before our great dinner. Board Chairman E. E. (Butch) McConner, Chairman of the Board. Wow! How great he and his lovely wife, Laney, with their 3 kids, Janice, Eddie and Steve were and still are. They have done and still do for First Methodist Church Attalla. Both gone to be with God.

In 1972 Judy Bostick started kindergarten with Lillian Clayton, teacher. 17 members. Judy came back to help us. Congressman Tom Bevill from Jasper, Alabama where my lovely wife, Iris is from, gave a U.S. flag that had been flown over capitol building in Washington, D. C. to kindergartners.

Sunday January 28, 1973 Bishop Carl Sanders dedicated Parsonage. Mortgage burned May 29, 1966. Open house new parsonage. Paid in 7 years thanks to all faithful members of First Methodist Attalla. Committee chairman, Gordon R. Isbell, Sr. gone to be with God. Mrs. Horace Banks, Mrs. C. R. Shepherd, John Lyons. Since gone Frank Ledbetter, L. B. Todd. Living George Hundley, Clarence Rhea, Dr. T. M.

Owens. Thanks to all of you on committee. You were just great.

1973 Committee to study to renovate educational building. Gordon R. Isbell, Jr. Ralph Culp, Mrs. Charles O'Rear. Deceased Mr. Frank Ledbetter, Bill Drake, James Glover, J. S. Robinson.

October 13, 1973 Lavinia Hunter and Banks classes hundred morning service. Mrs. Clarence Jones, Mrs. Ralph Brown, Mrs. Navorah, Little John, Miss Tera Trammel, Mrs. Nan Ellen Black, Mrs. Maggie Brothers, Mrs. Fred Cox, Mrs. P.L. Cameron, Mrs. William Cole, Mrs. Henry Culp, Mrs. Gordon R. Isbell, Sr., Mrs. J. E. Smith. All gone to be with God. Some great people of Attalla who helped make Attalla a great place to live.

Mr. James Ralph Brown had Brown Service Station downtown Attalla. Brown's Motel was behind it. It was a real fine motel. Roden Garage was behind service station owned by Walter Roden, son Leon, went all through school with Gordon R. Isbell, Jr. Good looking and the girls loved his looks. Mr. Brown was on every board in Attalla-Married Miss Willie Kate Wise from Hokes Bluff. What a leader she was also. Mrs. Brown, Mrs. Banks, Mrs. C. R. Shepherd, and my Mama, Mrs. Gordon R. Isbell, Sr. and Mrs. Clarence Mae Jones ran Youth Department at First Methodist Church. Over 250 in Sunday School - probably largest in city of Attalla. Mr. and Mrs. Brown lived at 609 Hughes Avenue, Attalla. They had 3 daughters Elaine Brown Ford (Hayden), Katherine Brown Burke (Louie) and Harriett Brown Burke (Bill).

Mr. George P. Walker, owner of Walker Drug Store in Attalla on the corner of 5th Avenue and 4th Street, married Mrs. Walker. They went to First Baptist church each Sunday. She walked direct with back and shoulders up. I would be at First Methodist Church and I would always holler out and say,

Good Morning. Mrs. Walker always had that beautiful smile, Good Morning Gordon, come to see me. Her daughter Mrs. Julia Walker Russell, husband Tom, owner Russell Mills in Alexander City. They had 2 daughters. Mrs. Julia taught me a speech when I was 4 years old—Wish I was a rock

Sitting on a hill

I would not eat

I would not sleep

But just sit and rest myself by gosh.

That is 76 years ago. I used to stop to see her when I was hitch-hiking to Auburn. I ate many meals with her family. It was raining so hard one Sunday she had her chauffeur to take me to Auburn to my Fraternity, Sigma Nu. When he got there the Chauffeur got out and opened the door for me and got my luggage for me. My fraternity brothers thought I was something. I never let them know the difference. Mrs. Julia and Mr. Tom Russell were always nice to me. Mrs. Tom (Julia Walker) had a building named after her at Huntington College in Montgomery, Alabama.

Daughter Bea married to Mr. Frank Shepard, cotton broker. Son Mr. George P. Walker, Jr. went to Auburn, Phi Delta Theta Fraternity. Graduated Auburn Pharmacy School, came back and ran Walker Drug Store. He was a big hunter and fisherman. Nice and great like Dr. George P. Walker, Sr. He married Miss Mildred Hearn from Albertville who was in charge of Library at Etowah High School. What a pretty lovely lady. Later she ran Attalla Library. When it was built new in Attalla I wanted the city to name it Mrs. George (Mildred) Walker, Jr. Library because she did so much for the library. They had 3 children, Dr. George P. Walker III, an outstanding doctor and he and his fine family live in Gadsden. Daughter,

Jane Walker Crow, married Warren Crow from Birmingham. Her Aunt (Mrs. Frank (Bea Walker) Shepard tried to get her to date me while I was in Auburn. Jane told her I was too old. I often kid Jane about me being too old to date her. Dr. George P. Walker, Sr. lived on the corner of 4th Street and 7th Avenue in Attalla. He would go pick up John Morris at the corner house on 5th Street and 7th Avenue. I think they named Morris High School after him. Dr. Walker, Sr. and John Morris picked me up as a little boy at 712 5th Street and took me to Dr. Walker's farm on old Boaz Highway. Close to the road where you turn right to go to Duck Springs. Dr. Walker let me pick apples and grapes, figs, peaches when in season. Uncle John Morris would take me to the creek and show me how to fish. I will never forget Dr.Walker and Uncle Morris. When I had my pony and buggy with my friend , Shenny Worthy, we would go to see Dr. Walker. He would always give me an ice cream cone. I love Dr. George Walker, Sr. I had Saturday morning program playing records, talking about Lily Pure ice cream. Dr. Walker never charged me for using upstairs building.

Mr. Walter Drake was a pharmacist at Walker Drug. Mrs. Drake taught school. They lived on 5th Ave next to Tucker. Mrs. Jewel taught me at grammar school - 3rd grade. She was so pretty and sweet to all us kids. Mr. and Mrs. Drake had a lovely daughter, Mary, who married Excel Hester who was a great football hero at Etowah High. Upstairs in the Walker Drug building, was Dr. S. C. Stutts, Dentist-lived on 5th Street where Dr. Pharr's office is now. Robert used to have office in Walker building. Dr. Stutts had two sons - S.C. went to Etowah High, then to Howard College Baptist School in East Lake Birmingham. I, Gordon R. Isbell, Jr. had the honor to be only Methodist to be president Royal Ambassador (RA) at First Baptist Church. Also President my church First Methodist Church at the same time. I used to visit S. C. Stutts at Howard College for RA convention. I would stay in S.C.Stutts ' room and he took me to my first cafeteria right off campus. People were nice to me and I will never forget S. C. Stutts. I used to deliver Dr. and Mrs. Stutts their Birmingham newspaper on my 26 inch bicycle. Across the street from Dr. Stutts lived Mr. Tony Edwards, who worked for my Daddy at Isbell and Hallmark Furniture Store next to Merchants and Farmers Bank. Mr. C. R. Shepherd owned the building.

Later Dr. T. M. (Mac) Owens had an office in Walker building. He and his lovely wife, Dixie, lived in the corner house of 3rd Ave. and 4th Street. They had 2 boys - Tommy and Jimmy.

On 3rd Avenue Mr. and Mrs. Charles Cooper lived. They had grocery store. Mr. Dooley had dry cleaners I believe next to Merchant and Farmers bank. When depression hit Daddy moved back to West Gadsden Store and Uncle Hal moved East Gadsden store to West Gadsden, where it is today and where we have been 98 plus years. Hill's grocery moved in building where Daddy was. Olive McDonald later married Bill Ellis in Dr. Walker's building. Next door Mr. J. J. Robertson Barber Shop - what a great man he was.

Paul Waters plumbing 3rd Street, Casey Jones 3rd Street worked Attalla Pipe Sop. He and Mrs. Jones supported all civic projects - raised Jimmie Dunlap plus Paul Harris who married Jewell Shirley who worked at Exchange Bank. Jewell went to our church before they died; Jewel was kin to Gerald and Callie Waldrop who had 2 daughters, one teaching in Birmingham, the other in Jasper working for Alabama school system. Up 3rd Street Kalevas Hotel as you take left to go to Attalla Pipe Shop where Mrs. Ethel Hendry worked, then became secretary of First Methodist Church Attalla, then Florence Little, daughter, took over. Up street Mr. and Mrs. Galman raised chickens -in church sat in right center section, 4th seat from front First United Methodist Church. They set an example for all of us. Mr. and Mrs. Galman - had a beautiful daughter, her husband use to coach at Etowah.

Clyde Burke was a foreman at Attalla Pipe Shop. Mrs. Burke, the greatest, I ate many meals at her house on Stowers Hill, 3rd Street Attalla. John James Burke, the oldest dated Elsie Leigh Banks for years. I dated Jane Banks. He would let us double date to go to picture show cause I was legally age to drive but got my driver's license at 13 years old. (Surely I did not misrepresent my age.) Guess I just looked older - Ha! John James married Helen from Arkansas. He worked Attalla Pipe Shop, went up ladder to Atlanta, then back to Birmingham. Daughter, Susan, married Dowd Ritter CEO of AmSouth Bank in Birmingham and all over. Louie and John James and Marvin went to Auburn, Sigma Nu Fraternity. Bill got off track and went to that other school in Tuscaloosa, I believe called Alabama where Martha Lou Jones plus Henry and Clarence Frost Rhea, Iris Taylor Johnson, Katherine Brown Burke did. Don't guess they could get in Cow College school, the great Auburn. Louie Burke worked at Allis Chalmers like Gordon R. Isbell, Jr. did in the summer. Married Katherine Brown Burke, went to Auburn. Marvin went to Etowah High School and Auburn. He became an accountant in Anniston, Ala. Sister Kitty and son, Frank, were other Clyde Burke children.

Garner and Opal Vann moved from Gadsden to Attalla. They were great members of First Methodist Church of Attalla. Wish all people could do what they have done for God and Church. They lived at 108 5th Ave Attalla. Garner was Post Office rural mail carrier, Opal had beauty parlor at rear of home. Garner started Vann Express in 1939-authorized to carry up to 60 lbs per item. They now live at 620 Line Street. Daughter Susan married Bob Sims, mother Mary Ruth Sims played organ at First Methodist for many years. Husband Ralph ran youth group. Susan and Bob had one daughter, Emily. She married Wes, two great children.

Mr. and Mrs. Homer Turner lived on 5th Avenue. Daughter Alice married David Walker, great friend. Some more fun people. We had good times. David made everyone he knew happy. Alice, a doll, Homer Jr. worked for Wood-Isbell Dance Hall. Took up money. Made big wages, 5 cents a night. Look at the good training and experience he got. Homer retired Vice President of Alabama Power - lives in God's country Auburn. Sister, Lucy, married Newman Nowlin.

Mr. and Mrs. Harris lived on Hughes Ave. across from Mr. and Mrs. Burke Phillips. The Harris' had a daughter, Marian, who married Heyward Millican and they had twin daughters who live on Stowers Hill, go to First Baptist Church; Marion still pretty as she always was. Mrs. Myrtle of 5th Avenue worked at Liberty Theater across the street from Walker Drug Store. Jack Brown was the manager, he would go to picture show, church, hunt, fish, and that is it. Chief of Police Glen Brown, Policeman Mr. Bill Keener, Policeman, Mr. A. B. Fowler, they used to check on Jimmie Wood and My dance hall every Friday night, never had a minute of trouble.

Mr. and Mrs. George Little, corner house 7th Avenue and 4th Street across from City Hall. Son George Little was oldest, then John, and sister (I always knew her as Sister Little). Frank Hawkins, 1st through 12th grade with me lives in Tuscaloosa. He had a brother, George, an attorney in Gadsden; his daddy worked for the Southern Railroad. Eva Edwards 1st street married Theo Strickett, had 2 sons, 1 in army, other went to Tulane University. Arvesta Edwards Holly Street-worked for Mama 50 years. Arvesta like a member of our family.

In Harry Hollar that North 5th Avenue North way North, Mrs. Minton had large family. Pinky great football player at Etowah; brother Roy very successful grocery and meat store Attalla, also car lot as well as sold vacuum cleaners.

Classmate Knowles Wilson made it big in Nashville, Tennessee. He made lots of money. Once when my 3 boys were at Baylor Prep School in Chattanooga, we took them to the Grand Ole Opry to see Red Leach's daughter, Clare, on stage. We called Knowles Wilson and he sure entertained my family. Goober was on stage; he went to school at Jasper High in Jasper, Alabama. Before the show started he was signing autographs. Iris went up behind him and hugged him. He jumped up in front of all those folks and danced on the table and started dancing with Iris. In the middle of his show he stopped and said would the prettiest girl in Jasper, Alabama, who he went to high school with, stand up. Iris' Daddy owned two picture shows in Jasper and let him sweep the floor and let him go to the show anytime. Goober took us to dinner. He came to Gadsden, stayed at the Reich Hotel. Put on a show at Gadsden State. Came to our home for refreshments. He told me "Gordon, you are the luckiest man living. You married the prettiest gal in Jasper." The whole town love her because she and her parents were so nice to everyone. His family didn't have a pot to put a pea in. I ate many meals at Iris Taylor Johnson's house. My friend of 63 years, Bill Harbert, from Birmingham and Joy Patrick Harbert and Iris are best of friends for 73 years. They were in Hollywood and called Goober. Nothing would do but for Bill and Joy to stay with Goober and his wife. Bill said he really wined and dined them...plus took them through all the studios where he made his movies. Several times he would call Iris and me to come see him and his wife. Goober was the same in person as he was on stage. Now wish we had gone. Children in Prep school too busy. I tell students never go to summer school unless flunking.

People didn"t have all the luxuries then as they do today. But bet most people then had good time. Wouldn't take anything for living in Attalla; never knew a bad person, black or white. No doors were ever locked. Everybody respected everybody and cared for others. Hobos often came to our house 2 ½ blocks from railroad. Mama would always try to feed them, make them go wash face and hands and say a prayer, asking God to bless them. Mama put them at the back porch table and I often ate with them. Many times she let them spend the night in garage apartment. If it was a Saturday Daddy would make them clean up and go to Sunday School or Church with us and sit with us. Often Daddy gave them a clean shirt and pants and made them polish their shoes. He gave them 10 cents to give to God when collection plate passed by. Daddy always gave a dollar bill. When they left many hobos often came back to see us - even clean our yard.

I thank God often for the honor to have been raised in Attalla. I knew everyone and they knew me. They wanted to help me. When I was selling bedspreads, blankets, dress length material, pots, pans, even lending $1.00 per week, pay me back one dollar and ten cents Next Saturday very few didn't pay me back. I loaned a colored man $1.00 one week and he couldn't pay me back the next $1.10, the next week he owed me $1.20, wouldn't pay. Sunday morning 3 of his friends brought him to our back porch. He paid me, said he was sorry; he said his friends were going to whip him unless he paid you, Mr. Gordon. He and his wife still trade with me.

On Sunday you need to go to Sunday School and church. Don't forget the Lord because only expect 10% of your Net, other wise if you make $1.00, give God 10 cents. Try it, God will bless you, I know because God has blessed me with a great Mama, Daddy, a lovely wife, Iris, and 3 great sons and a daughter-in-law and 6 wonderful grandchildren. Amen.

Memories

---Paschal Means

The city of Attalla was incorporated as a town on February 5, 1872 by Alabama Legislature. Andrew Jackson established a food supply camp on the banks of Big Wills Creek where Rhea's Lake was later located. The present water works of the City of Attalla is now located there.

In 1903 Attalla became the first town in the United States to be lighted with hydroelectric power. W. P. Lay, a river boat captain, while watching the water rushing through the flume and water wheel at lock 2 on the Coosa River, conceived the idea of making water turn a dynamo. After traveling in the United States and Europe, he returned home and obtained the old Wesson Mill on Big Wills Creek. After rebuilding the dam and obtaining leases from land owners in Big Wills Valley to flood part of their land, he installed a 75 horsepower capacity turbine-driven generator. Mr. Lay's agreement with the town of Attalla would furnish free power to the town in exchange for a franchise to install electric power in home and businesses in the town. On Dec. 6, 1906 the Alabama Power Company was incorporated from this endeavor.

By 1912 Captain Lay passed control of the power company to James Mitchell and the power plant was moved from Big Wills Creek to Coosa River. At that time Captain Lay said "I now commit to you the good name and destiny of The Alabama Power Company. May it be developed for the service of Alabama." From this agreement the City of Attalla still receives free power for lights in all buildings belonging to the city, such as public schools and city hall.

My father, Paschal Porter Means, Sr., was one of the first lineman employed by Alabama Power Co. He worked for the company over 40 years. His nickname was "Boss Man."

References: History of Attalla, First Baptist Church book, Records from Alabama Power Company

History Of The Charles Washington McElroy Family In Attalla, Alabama

Around 1919 Charles Washington McElroy, wife Annie Tate McElroy and only child Charles Bernard McElroy, moved to Attalla from Cuba, Alabama after selling his house and woodworking business.

His cousin Dr. Jim McElroy was responsible for this move by telling him of the wonderful advantages of living in Attalla. A new box factory was being built and the mills were employing extra people, increasing the size and production. Charles Washington opened a new business called Quality Shoe Repair.

His son Charles Bernard graduated from Etowah High School, married Pauline Loner from Alabama City and worked in the shoe industry for a number of years before becoming a postal employee in Gadsden.

Bernard and Pauline McElroy had two children. Dr. James Bernard McElroy was the first Cardiologist at Baptist Montclair in Birmingham, Alabama. He married Karen Andersen and they had the following three children: James Bernard, Jr.; Jeanie; and Betsy. Robert George McElroy had Heath-McElroy Insurance Agency in Gadsden for forty years. He married Bette Sue Bobo. Their two children are Mary Ann and Robert George, Jr.

Attalla, Alabama As It Was

by Clarence Rhea

Clarence F. Rhea was born in Attalla, Alabama 21 August 1921

William Henry Rhea and wife, Elvela Frost Rhea, parents of Clarence Frost Rhea had nine children born at 207 4th Street Attalla, Alabama and six of the nine children survived viz: William Henry Rhea, Jr.; Clarence Frost Rhea, married Marie Cannon; Elvela Frost Rhea (Roden), married Bill Roden, Richard Eugene Rhea, married Martha Jane Bain, Martha Frances Rhea (Mitchell) married Joe Mitchell, Anna Margaret Rhea (Knight) married Melvin Knight.

Mrs. Beaird (Jean Williams grandmother) helped my mother at the births of each child.

Captain Rufus Rhea lived at Lake Rhea and Lamont Nicholson wrote that Rufus Rhea came to Attalla 6 days a week and took back one quart of whiskey. He is buried in the cemetery lot at Oak Hill Cemetery in Attalla, Alabama.

Section One

Yankee Troops captured Rhea at bridge over Big Wills

Grandfather William Henry Rhea was born in 1846. He was kicked out of the Confederate Army due to being only 15 years' old. His brother, Rufus Rhea, was a Captain and commanded a troop of Confederate Calvary.

At age 15, while he and John Noble were fishing in May of 1861, from the bridge to Lake Rhea, my grandfather was captured by Yankee troops led by Col. Streight. Rhea and Noble heard horses. John Noble said "sounds like Yankees" but William Rhea said "No, it's the Confederate calvary of my brother Rufus." Noble escaped but Rhea was captured. When he saw the flood at Black Creek, Streight took some burning embers from the Sansom home and burned the bridge across Black Creek. He took the brother of Emma Sansom, who was a wounded Confederate soldier convalescing at his sister's hoe, and escaped ahead of Gen. Nathan Bedford Forrest.

Emma Sansom rode behind General Forrest to show him a place to cross Black Creek. At midnight Forrest caught 1600 Yankees with Col. Streight about 6 miles above Cedar bluff on the way to Rome, Georgia.

Forrest had only 500 Confederate soldiers and two cannons. He was able to confuse Streight and caused him to surrender his 1600 men. The 400 southern men that were with Col. Streight had refused to fight for the South and were branded by the Southerners as guilty of treason and not subject to being swapped.

Clarence F. Rhea's great-grand-grandfather, Louis L. Rhea, was born in 1797 in Tennessee. He fought in the War of 1812 with Andrew Jackson and was discharged in 1814. Following the Battle of New Orleans he walked back to

Tennessee and passed thru Attalla, Alabama stopping a few days at the Holloway home near what is now Lake Rhea. He returned about ten years later and married a Holloway girl. Both are buried at Shiloh Cemetery near St. Clair County Line off Highway 11.

Louis Rhea received a patent from President Polk for 40 acres of land the east line of which is now downtown Gadsden. Two years later he sold the 40 acres for $200.00.

Section Two

Cost five cents to ride the street car from Attalla to Gadsden

A street car from Gadsden turned around at the AGS RR station in Attalla and stopped for a passenger in front of our house. For five cents we could ride one mile to my grandfather's, Clarence Miller Frost, house at 505 Hughes Avenue in Attalla, Alabama or could, for the same nickel, ride to Gadsden.

Section Four

Homing Pigeons Flew from Attalla to Kentucky

In the1920's and early 1930's some Lexington, Kentucky businessmen shipped several crates of homing pigeons to Attalla. Dad and his children released the pigeons at the AGS Railroad Station at dawn (about 5:00 a.m.) in Attalla and the pigeons flew back to their home in Lexington, Kentucky.

Section Five

White Robed Men

In the middle 1920's a long line of white robed men marched from town down 4th Street and when I expressed concern, Dad took me to the sidewalk and we watched as those persons passed by with practically no sound and later about a mile away a large cross burned on a hill near a road to Boaz.

My older brother, William Henry Rhea, Jr., and I rode to Pennsylvania with a first cousin, "Pete" Frost, his mother and younger sister and visited Washington, D. C. and Valley Forge and many other places in and about Philadelphia and the Delaware River that Washington crossed near Trenton, New Jersey. We accompanied Uncle Frank Frost to purchase a St. Bernard puppy and it rode back to Attalla with us. The dog was called "Major."

Section Six

Major lived on vegetables and "left over meat"

A large vacant lot (now owned by the Attalla Church of Christ) was then used as a large garden to grow beans, peas, corn, radishes, lettuce, and cucumbers and many other vegetables. On Saturday night Uncle Frank visited the grocery stores in Attalla including A&P, Hills, Coopers,etc. and for 25cents or less, purchased meat to put in the large vats of "vegetables." The dog, "Major," grew very large.

About 1931 a large black dog called Prince (owned by L. B. Todd) harassed "Major." It was discovered with its head in "Major's" mouth. Major was full grown and "Mac," the gardener, helped Uncle Frank quickly extract the head of the Todd dog from the mouth of "Major."

Uncle Frank and "Mac" tested "Major" as to his ability to save someone from drowning. This was done in Little Wills Creek at Trestle Bend, a place many Attalla boys used for swimming. Mac jumped in the creek. He started yelling. The dog jumped in to save Mac but only left him badly mauled and

113

scared. That ended the effort of Frank Frost and Mac to train the St. Bernard to drag persons from a stream.

Complaints were made by several persons in downtown Attalla about the short red headed man and the dog "as big as a horse" that walked downtown (1930-1931.)

My Mother wrote many letters to her brother, Eugene, in Ardmore, Pa. and referred to the dog "Major" as a disgrace in eating large quantities of food when numbers of people with children were hungry. We hated to see the dog returned to Philadelphia.

William Henry Rhea, Sr. and son, William Henry Rhea, Jr. and C. F. Rhea took the small rails and wheels with broken flanges which were used by the ore mines in Attalla and wood obtained at a heading mill at Five Points Attalla in about 1933, and built a small train with iron wheels and assembled it in the vacant lot next to our house at 207 4th Street, Attalla.

We "fashioned" an elevated train about 8 to 10 feet high using a few steel rails and steel. Pieces of wood were used to build a train with maybe a 10% grade and the train would go very fast on approximately 100 feet of track and the last 50 feet was grass and the ground was packed by use. Many people enjoyed riding the "wooden railroad." The fun increased each time the train ran off the track.

Mrs. William Henry Rhea lived at 201 North 4th Street Attalla and had a deep well at the back of her house and during each "dry spell" many families, both white and black, and many children came to Grandma's house from late each afternoon throughout the night to obtain water.

No one ever took fruit such as figs, grapes or pomegranates and were very careful to speak only in whispers so as not to interfere with the rest and sleep of Grandma Rhea (who died in February 1941) and her daughter and teacher, Martha Clementine Rhea (who died in December 1980.)

George Hawkins, Jr. gave his Birmingham Post paper route to my brother, Henry, and the 12 customers, if all paid, generated 72 cents profit after paying 72 cents to the Birmingham Post people. My brother decided I was capable of delivering the newspapers. By hard work I increased the circulation and won a trip by railroad to Pensacola, Florida. Each of us paid 15 cents for a "miniature" bottle of alcohol beverage. This was the only thing we could acquire with our limited means.

A Reverend Johnson lived next to Walker's Lake. He let me drive his T-Model Ford as payment for about 36 cents that he owed for papers. Grandpa Frost in about 1930 permitted me to drive him home from the freight station (about ½ mile) to 505 Hughes Avenue. My grandfather was paralyzed on his left side but he felt that at 9 years of age I should be driving and he could give me instructions. I could not see where we were going and constantly slipped lower in the seat and we had a very rough ride. When we got to 505 Hughes Avenue seven grownups were there and furious at me and Grandpa.

Hudspeth and Berry Connection

William Henry Rhea, my grandfather, had a sister named Martha Frances Rhea Berry. Her daughter was the founder of Berry College in Rome, Georgia. Martha Berry, two or three times a year, would spend one week visiting with her sister-in-law, Mrs. Henry Rhea, en route to her home in Mentone, Alabama.

Hudspeth was the name of grandmother Frost, i.e. Mrs. Clarence Miller Frost, who lived at 505 Hughes Avenue, Attalla, Alabama.

1943 After OCS (Officer Candidate School)

B. Todd at Fort Stewart, Georgia was the first soldier saluting 2nd Lt. C. F. Rhea in January1944. March 1944 - Clarence Frost Rhea, 2nd Lt. Sent to Fort Benning, Georgia for Infantry Training. December 1944 Rhea was at Camp Blanding, Florida when he received orders to Europe.

He was on the Queen Mary with 15,000 others which landed at Gronock, Scotland, then traveled by train to South Hampton, then by boat to LeHavre, France. Rhea's unit traveled over 250 miles and arrived May 1945 at the Elbe River 30 miles from Berlin. A Kraut soldier refused medical treatment for a wound until he spoke to a "man from Alabama." This Prussian "Hans Von Pustua" had bought cotton in Attala and knew Leon Locklear, Bat Kelley and Charles Shephard. When I identified myself to him, he told me that he had bought cotton in Alabama, including Attalla, and Dothan. In Attalla Von Pustea said that he became a friend of and knew Leon Locklear (pharmacist) at Stewart Drug Store and Bat Kelley, cotton buyer with a warehouse on Third Street and with Charlie Shepard, cotton broker in Gadsden, Alabama.

CONCLUSION: INFORMATION TO BE INCLUDED AND POSSIBLY OF INTEREST

Attalla was a main and principal stop by the railroads. Railroads were important to the success and growth of the City of Attalla. The AGS Railroad (Alabama Great Southern) had its intersection in Attalla with the L. & N. (Louisville and Nashville.) Several families in Attalla were active in the railroad (primarily the AGS). The Hinton family (including Mr. Hinton, sons Sidney Hinton,Tommy Hinton and George Hinton) were employed in maintaining the rail lines, cross ties and track bed. The Overstreet family (including Mr. Overstreet and the several sons) had a long history as engineers and other numerous jobs.

Clarence Miller Frost was an agent for many years of the AGS Railroad. He was also the agent for the Railway Express Agency. He was the grandfather of Clarence Frost Rhea and had several children. Members of the Clarence Miller Frost family who worked on the railroad included his sons and son-in-law; William Henry Rhea, Eugene Frost, Edwin Frost, Clarence Frost and Frank Frost. Clarence Miller Frost married Anna Livinia Hudspeth. The sons of Clarence Miller Frost and Anna L. Husdpeth Frost were Eugene Frost, Edwin Frost, Clarence Frost and Frank Frost. The daughters of Clarence Miller Frost who were born at 505 Hughes Avenue, Attalla, Alabama including the following: Eloise Frost (Mrs. Alto V.) Lee, Evelyn Frost (who died while a student at Randolph Macon College in Lynchburg, VA), Elvela Frost (Mrs. William Henry) Rhea, Eliza Jane Snow (daughter of Asiel Snow) of Snowville, VA. married George Washington Frost. She is buried on the Frost lot at Oakhill Cemetery.

A prominent Attalla business man was: B. C. O'Rear - grandfather

B.C. O'Rear owned a furniture store in Attalla

Mr. O'Rear had three sons and a daughter viz:

Jim O'Rear

Bud O'Rear

George W. O'Rear was an Admiral in the Navy and is a member of the Patriots Hall of Honor

Ruth O'Rear

A grandson of B. C. O'Rear, Hon. Charles O'Rear, 2004 Mayor of Attalla

Dr. T.M. Owens

Dr. T. M. Owens, when a student at the University of Alabama, was Fed at Graduate Hall. He and Clarence Frost Rhea each had a free room by serving as monitors in separate dormitories at The University of Alabama campus as monitors. Rhea set fire to the mattress (in the room he was occupying) to eliminate the infestation of bed bugs.

Joe and Ben Noojin - Brokers

Joe and Ben Noojin were the sons of J. E.Noojin. Joe and his sons were builders and hardware owners.

Back Row: Katherine Cole Frame, Gordon Isbell, Jr., Martha Lou Riddle
Seated: Dudley Frame

BACK ROW MAE JONES, ELSIE ~~~~~~~~~~~~~~~~
NELLE TURNER, CAROLYN CULP, MAY COLE, MARY FOWLER
FANNIE ISELL, Ruby Sue ~~~~

UNDINE WILLIAMS, KATE BROWN, MARY FRENCH   1943

ELSIE BANKS   MAE JONES   KATE BROWN   BELLE SHEPHERD 196

119

KATHERINE COLE, ELSIE LEIGH BANKS, GAYNELL

MARTHA LOU JONES—SEATED INEZ PUTMAN JULIA Philips

KATHERINE COLE   MARTHA LOU RIDDLE   KATHERINE DIXE BROWN BURKE
        FRAME   1947

Vivian Mae Brown
James Ralph Brown

GRADUATES OF ETOWAH COUNTY HIGH SCHOOL 1914

VIVIAN MAE BROWN LEFT BACK ROW

The Good Life beginning in Attalla, Alabama on April 29, 1921.

Martha Lou Jones Riddle

Once upon a time there was a baby girl born April 29, 1921 to Vivian Mae Brown Jones and Clarence Foster Jones in Attalla, Alabama. The house I grew up in had a big front porch which was wonderful for riding a kiddy car. In front of the house there was a sidewalk but the extra wide street in front was gravel. The sidewalk in front was splendid for skating and town to the east of 422 Fifth Avenue was only ½ block away.

Attalla was made up of two main streets. Fifth Avenue was the widest with street car tracks laid east for five miles to Gadsden, Alabama through which flowed the Coosa River. Between Attalla and Gadsden was Alabama City, home of Dwight Cotton Mills and Republic Steel. In Attalla on the north side of the city block was the two story Hammond Hotel as well as a shoe shop, Alabama Power Company office, small grocery store run by the Chergotakos family and at the end was the only brick building—the two story Attalla Bank.

Continuing east for ½ block there were no buildings but railroad tracks for the AGS—Alabama Great Southern railroad

123

from Chattanooga, Tennessee to Meridan, Mississippi. The watchman who stopped the traffic when a train was on the track was a one legged man named Charley Campbell. In stopping traffic he held up a wooden sign signifying a train crossing - **X**. Here on the south side of Fifth Avenue was the freight office for the AGS and a huge grassy parking area...for a few cars and wagons pulled by horses and mules bringing fresh produce to town on Saturdays. I've often walked home with a watermelon under each arm.

On the south side of the town block of Attalla at the west end of Fifth Avenue was Walker Drug Store. Up a set of stairs was Dr. Stutts' dental office and "Central" - who manned the telephone switchboard and who answered "Number Please" and then she would pull the cord from the number calling and connect it to the number being called. Often "Central" would know many folks plans and if the person was not at home, she would simply tell the caller. "Oh she's not at home, she's gone to visit Mrs. McDonald. After Walker Drug Store was the A & P Grocery Store, then DuPre Hardware and Lumber Company, who once had the Funeral Parlor. Then an office building and next Stewart Drug Store. Both drug stores had soda fountains, a pharmacy, and drug supplies like hair nets and shampoo and there was plenty of business for both. The next store was Block's Department Store, (Max and Izzy Block, the owners, once lived upstairs at my house.) Next was a furniture store probably O'Rear's and then on the corner of Fifth Avenue and Third Street was Lowi's who sold notions (thread and materials) and lots of spool cabinets that were fascinating.

Attalla had another town street that was Fourth Street running north and south. On the east side was Walker Drug Store, then a hardware store , grocery store, and further down the block, the newly built brick Attalla Post Office. Most often the Postmaster was a Democrat but occasionally there was a Republican Post Master. Across from Walker's was The

Picture Show., Liberty Theater. Bargain day was Wednesday afternoon when a child could go to the picture show for 10 cents and receive a coupon, which for another 10 cents one could buy a soda at Walker's Drug Store. My favorite was a cherry soda.

Next to the picture show was a café with a tile floor, then another grocery store, Hill's. Near the alley there was once Cooper's grocery store. Then several other stores completed the west side of Attalla's second block.

The population must have been about 4,000. The two main industries were Walworth Pipe and Foundry Co., south about a mile from town on Third Street, and then left across the railroad tracks and Compress Buckle Co., north about 1/3 of a mile on Third Street. I remember also that there was a blacksmith, Raymond Page on Fourth Avenue across Fourth Street. Often I was entertained by watching him shoe a horse or mule or pony. It was fascinating to see the bellows produce a red hot fire, then mold the horse shoe with his hammer ringing, and then nail it to the horse's hoof.

For recreation and entertainment the men in Attalla had a Gun Club for shooting clay pigeons from two towers. The shooter shouted "Pull" and a clay pigeon sailed out of one of the towers. Lots of skill and fun was involved for the shooter didn't know which side the clay pigeon was coming from. There was a two story clubhouse with a ballroom with benches around each side and there must have been a kitchen and bathroom. The men used the downstairs for storing their guns and equipment. Often we would go as a family and Mother would take a picnic to share with others. Great excitement to watch the men shoot!

Then there was the time that Berney Fowler and I decided to clip the hair on his white Spitz dog to make him look like a lion. We weren't much good with the scissors, and his dog didn't look at all like a lion, and to say that his Mother, Mrs. Fowler, was unhappy was to put it mildly.

To me the crowning spot of Attalla was Lake Rhea—part paved road and then a dusty road into the country where Lake Rhea was located. A tiny stream fed into a large swimming area with bath-houses for men and women and an open dance floor and concession stand on one side and on the other side were many picnic tables. Each family brought their own picnic supper and usually went in swimming beforehand. There was no charge for dancing except to feed the juke box but we did have to pay to go in swimming. Dorothy and Louise Cole were the most in demand for dancing partners and I thought it great fun just to hang over the rail and watch all the couples on the dance floor. Often Clarence Frost Rhea and I would walk to Lake Rhea (about 3 miles) and go swimming. Sometimes Katherine Cole Frame and I (after we were 16) would go out to Lake Rhea driving in a car for a morning swim, and then cook breakfast. Katherine liked only the yellow of the eggs and her Mother saved the whites for angel food cake.

There was heaps of excitement in Attalla when the Lamont Nicholson family came visiting. Lamont Nicholson was my Mother's Uncle and close friend who lived in Argentina and drove an automobile with the steering wheel on the right side. About every 3 years The Nicholsons visited our family when they came to the States to pick up their new automobile. Uncle Lamont was the younger brother of my Grandmother, Hattie F. Nicholson, and there was a room upstairs in our house that was always referred to as Monty's room. Uncle Lamont never liked his name. He said that his Mother was reading a book and liked the name Lamont. (I don't believe that he ever liked the name Vivian either.) But my Mother (Vivian Mae) had his name and it made her very happy because Uncle Lamont was special.

Uncle Lamont and Aunt Mary had three sons just a twit younger then I and it was pure heaven when they came visiting. One time when they were in Attalla the three Nicholson sons went downtown to have their hair cut at the barber shop. After the barber finished I sat in the chair and asked for the same type of haircut. I was 12 years old at that time and My Mother was hardly prepared for my boyish very short hair cut. I liked it!

Once Katherine Cole was sick and in bed and my Father and I had gone fishing (I paddled the boat, he fished) and he caught a huge bass which he kept alive until we could take the fish to Katherine. We watched it swim in her bathtub.

Most of the time I didn't wear shoes as I liked to go barefoot and play in my sand-pile which was next to the sidewalk between two oak trees. Outstanding was my 5th birthday party when my Mother and Daddy must have invited almost every 5 year old in town. Mr. Charley Griffin, the town photographer made a picture of all of us sitting on the front steps of my house. It does help to have pictures to remember all my friends. As an only child, friends were really important.

Across the street from my house was an apartment building, owned by Maw Childers, a widow, and where my friends Evelyn Childers and (Paul) Rastus Killian lived. Next door to them was a large two story house where Aunt Sally White lived. I never knew her husband; I think he was a Confederate veteran. I once spent the night there and slept in a feather bed. Aunt Sally had a car, perhaps a Model T Ford, but she wasn't much of a driver. Once she couldn't remember how to stop her car and approach her steep driveway so she kept driving around the block and when she reached Fifth Avenue she started calling for my Father, "Clarence, Clarence." He finally jumped on the running board of the car and got Aunt Sally safely up the driveway.

The next door neighbor of Aunt Sally was the Warren White's, whose wife was known as Miss Pearl. One of their children was named William and he was the town plumber. He didn't have a car so he took his tools in a wheelbarrow. I heard that when he was plumbing and wanted to hang his coat up, he just put a nail in the wall. He was an excellent plumber though.

From my Mother's porch swing she used to speak to everyone who was going to town. "Miss" Marietta Cox was a close friend and wore high heels and carried an open umbrella as she walked from her home on Fifth Street to Fifth Avenue to downtown Attalla. Miss Marietta, born in Mississippi told my Mother that she had worn high heels since she was 13. Her daughter, Mary Elizabeth was a friend of mine. Mary Elizabeth's Dad, Mr. Fred, and Miss Marietta, moved from Attalla for a while but later after Mr. Fred died, Miss Marietta and Mary Elizabeth Litty, husband Bill and children returned to Attalla.

Then there was Preacher Henry who quoted the bible as he walked to town. He was the town fix-it person and gardener. And he was a whiz at fixin' most anything. If my Mother was sitting in her swing as Preacher Henry went by, he always responded with a verse of scripture.

Our grammar school was a large brick two story building on East First Street across town where My Mother had gone to school. It was not a bad walk, about ½ mile but I did have to cross the railroad tracks. You can bet I paid special attention to Uncle Charley and his railroad stop sign. In fact I looked forward to entering first grade because I already knew the teacher, Lurleen O'Brien. In fact I believe that she lived upstairs at our house for my Mother and Father had rooms to rent, mainly to school teachers but with no meals included. There were four bedrooms upstairs and my Father had added a bath to each bedroom for the closets were very large and a shower, lavatory and toilet could fit in easily and still leave room for clothes to hang.

Anyhoo school was fun and recess was thrilling. One of the teachers, Mrs. French who also had lived at our house, played the piano as we gathered in the auditorium. One day in the 6th grade some of the old plaster fell on our teacher, Mrs. Guest, and we thought it was funny. She didn't.

So the years passed and I finished 8th grade in the old building.

In 1933 my Father had a 7 passenger Cadillac and my Mother decided to drive to the World's Fair in Chicago. She chose 5 friends from Attalla to go with us and this was a tremendous driving education course because there were no traffic lights in Attalla and very few automobiles. The trunk for our car was a real black trunk which held 3 black flat rectangular suit cases and was strapped on a rack at the back of the car. There were two jump seats in the middle of the car so since I was the only child, I was relegated to ride on one of the jump seats the whole way. The other passengers traded about after a number of miles. The trip was a huge success, there was no car trouble (which was a miracle), the World's Fair was stupendous and we all had a good time.

Three years later in 1936 My Mother had a new Pontiac and she chose three friends (her sister-in-law, Kate Brown, Mae Cole, and Dorothy Howell, (a friend who lived in Gadsden) to drive to Mexico and be gone a month. I went to stay with my cousins, Elaine, Katherine Mae, and Harriet and their Father, Uncle Ralph. They had a cook. Uncle Ralph took us to Daytona Beach for a vacation.)

The Pan-American highway had just opened and with no one speaking Spanish, the four Alabama women from Attalla drove to Mexico City which included Taxco, Cuernavaca,

Xochimilco, etc. I think they drove 3600 miles and no car trouble—another miracle. (See May Cole's Journal in this same book.)

High School was Etowah County High School, the first high school in Etowah County in 1909 and also where My Mother had graduated in 1914 in a class of 5. I had a sidewalk all the way and walked the 1 ½ miles every day unless it rained and then my Mother drove me in her car to school. It didn't rain very often. School at Etowah was different because the students moved from room to room and most of the teachers had home rooms. The gymnasium was in a wooden building with hundreds of steps (seemed like) down the hill. I was especially fond of the gym teacher, Ruth Stephens, so I not only took my required gym class, but used my study halls to take extra classes at the gym.

Since Etowah was a County School about half the student body came on busses from various parts of the county. These students started in the 7th grade. Our school didn't teach biology but we had a terrific math teacher, Maud Floyd Herndon who saw that our class had available classes in Beginning Algebra, Advanced Algebra, Geometry, and some Trig. (Well that was almost my undoing because when I enrolled at the University of Alabama in 1939 as a freshman, I was put in an advanced Junior math class.) I didn't fail but almost!

In Attalla our two churches First Methodist and First Baptist were friends. On Sunday nights we had the traditional evening service one Sunday with the Methodist and the next with the Baptist. Bible School was also traded each year. The First Methodist Church was on the corner of Sixth Avenue and Fourth Street (still is) and the First Baptist Church was a block to the west on the corner of Sixth Avenue and Fifth Street, still there. The church families were strong and faithful and we never missed a Sunday going to church as well as Wednesday night. When My Mother was Superintendent of the Junior Department we had lots of picnics and hikes—once I remember we walked several miles to a Spring up Highway 11. My friend, Faye Keener, whose Mother was the soloist for the choir, and My Mother who sang in the choir, were in charge of the Christmas pageant one year. They decided on blue sheets for a sky background in the choir loft. No colored sheets were available so Miss Ruby Sue and My Mother dyed their white sheets blue and Faye and I slept on blue sheets for years. Speaking of Faye, her Mother was in charge of communion so every first Sunday I went home with Faye who lived across the street from the church, and we finished drinking all the grape juice that was left in the communion cups.

Three of us, Katherine Templin Cole Frame, and Dorothy Eloise Tarpley (Oh yes double names were the vogue) and I had ponies. Katherine's pony was Dixie, Dot's pony was Nancy, and my pony was Prince. Each of us had a tiny stable behind our houses and our ponies were our pride and joy. One Christmas my Mother had a dressmaker to make me a blue corduroy riding habit complete with a matching blue cap. It was great to ride together and to look after our ponies.

I was lucky also to have a horse, Reba, for a year. My Mother's friend, Dorothy Howell in Gadsden owned Reba and loaned us her horse for a year. We already had the stable so I cared for Reba, who was a Black Beauty, and I rode her most every afternoon. There were small mountains to the west where the ore mines were and beyond there was farm land with several creeks. Reba liked roaming around on the dirt roads and I was grateful and happy to ride as well as look after her.

For entertainment seven girls formed a Club and we had spend-the-night parties. They were fun also. Besides Katherine and Dot, there was Elsie Leigh Banks, Julia Varina Phillips, Sidney Kathryn Williams, Mary Faye Keener, and me.

Later when we were in high school each of us chose a boy and we had a Club that met every Friday night. The boys took their turn also at being the host and thus we had something to look forward to each week.

Etowah County High School didn't have a band and our football team didn't win many games but we cheered for them never- the- less. The game we really wanted to win was to beat "Gadsden" -a much larger city about 5 miles east, but that didn't happen very often. Several years later after our class of 1939 had graduated and when Coach Glover came to Etowah, it was another story. Etowah started winning!

The most outstanding social event at Etowah was the annual Junior-Senior banquet held at the Reich Hotel in Gadsden. My date as a Senior was Kenneth Alfred Riddle who would be attending Auburn University. We dated, kept in touch through the years after he graduated from Auburn in Electrical Engineering and I received my degree from the University of Alabama in Personnel Management in 1943. Ken went immediately into the Army and to Officer Training School at Fort Belvoir while I accepted a job in the Accounting Department of Tennessee Eastman Corporation at Oak Ridge, Tennessee. We became engaged in November 1946 and married in Attalla on June 14, 1947 at the Attalla First Methodist Church. Happiness was in store for us for over 50 years. He died of emphysema in October 1997.

Our graduating Class of 1939 has been outstanding because it hasn't forgotten Etowah. Clarence Frost Rhea, now an attorney in Gadsden and who has been our Chairman for 64 years so we're going to keep him for forever. He called our first Class Reunion at our 25th Reunion in 1964. It was my Mother's 50th and she came also. A large attendance out of our class of 79 were present and we met in the school cafeteria. At a later gathering, perhaps our 30th it was suggested that each class member give $250 toward a scholarship fund;

the interest of such fund to be awarded yearly to the most outstanding student of the Senior Class at Etowah who would be attending college. When Roger Holmes died tragically and later his wife, Dorothy Eloise Tarpley Holmes died, she left a large bequest to the Class of 1939 Scholarship Fund. Also through the years the Class of 1939 has continued to add to this fund. It has grown considerably...now in 2004 it has grown to $27,262.82 in C.D.'s and $297.12 in savings. The Award of the Class of 1939 now amounts to $1000.00. each graduation year. Lorraine Harris Whitt and Jeanette Hamrick Thornhill have been so faithful to telephone classmates when its Reunion time. Mary Frances Gaines Hollingsworth, Harold Overstreet and Henry Graham have given generously of their time in presenting The Class of 1939 award for our class. The Class of 1939 has met for its 25th, 30th, 35th, 40th, 45th, 50th, then yearly since 1989. It is Clarence Frost Rhea who is our guiding light and has kept us together with constant reminders of class news and reunions. Charles Franklin Rowan and Harold Overstreet are the dedicated members who plan the Reunions. Oh yes, some years ago we changed from night to noon meetings.

Ken and I lived in Sharon, Pennsylvania for 6 years while he worked for Westinghouse in designing large transformers. Two of our sons, Jesse Douglas Riddle II, and Ralph Krannert Riddle were born in Sharon. We moved to Rome, Georgia in August 1953 where Ken accepted a job in Engineering with Georgia Kraft Co., now Temple-Inland Corporation. Our third son, Alfred Nicholson Riddle, was born in Rome.

Life goes on with its many wonderful surprises and Rome, Georgia is indeed a stimulating town in which to live. Of course its people make it so. Ken died in October of 1997 but Doug and Elaine and their son, Jess, live in Roswell, Georgia, Kran and Jody and daughter, Chelsea, and son, Zach, are in Savannah and Alfy and his wife, Glenda, are in California. We see each other often and in the meantime I continue to count my many blessings which include all of you whom I have known and loved.

Attalla, The Early Days: The Thirties and Forties

- Lorraine Harris Whitt b. May 19, 1921

The name Attalla is an Indian name meaning "Home." That is a very appropriate name for those of us who have called Attalla home over the years.

In the thirties and forties we had an electric streetcar that ran from Gadsden to Attalla. It came down Fifth Avenue, turned left onto Fourth Street, and turned around on Third Street. When Cleveland Avenue was made a four-lane highway, we had a regular bus that ran from Attalla to Gadsden.

Attalla was a railroad center where the Southern, the L & N, and the NC Saint L came through. The freight depot was located on Third Street. The train station was located two blocks down on Third Street. Folks came from many places to catch the train there.

Mrs. Ira Harris had the first dress shop in town. It was located on Fifth Avenue. When her lease ran out, she had no place to go because a big five and ten cent store was coming in and taking the space of three buildings. Later Mrs. Paul

Bone and Coleen Bone put in a dress shop on Fourth Street. It was named Bone's Dress Shop.

Mr. Grover Gilliland ran a gristmill that was located on Fourth Avenue. His big hat was always covered with white meal. John Coffee ran a blacksmith shop, which was located on Fourth Avenue. On Saturday, the farmers would come to town in their rigs (mules and wagons) to do their trading. They would park in the large space behind the stores and while they were there, they would have their mules shod as well as other jobs. There was another blacksmith shop that was owned by Raymond Page in the parking area.

The Ed Bynum family ran a mule barn on Third Street. Lots of mule trading was done there. Hazel Holland had the first beauty shop in town. It was located on Fifth Avenue. Ruth Barkley had a beauty shop on Fourth Street. Helene King later put in a beauty shop located behind George P. Walker's drug store. There were four doctors in town. Dr. E. K. Hamby was the Attalla Pipe Shop family doctor. The other doctors were Dr. Rowan, Dr. McElroy, and Dr. Stewart who lived on Fifth Avenue.

Mr. Francis Reed owned and operated a large mercantile store on Fourth Street. He sold everything from spools of thread to cow feed. There was a large pot bellied stove in the back of the store where the bus drivers would congregate until school was out. They would eat their lunch there, consisting of cheese and crackers and sardines.

Miss Ida Hamner owned the building at the corner of Fourth Street and Fourth Avenue. Her brother, Ed Hamner, ran a store there. It is said that he wore a long tail-coat and a high top hat and carried an umbrella on his arm. When he got to the store he would put on an apron. In the same block there was a filling station owned by Mr. Ralph Brown. He later moved across the street and added a garage and a motel. There was also Culp's Iron and Metal on the same block. They later moved out on the Lake Rhea Road. Lake Rhea was a popular place in the thirties, where lots of young people would go on Saturday night to dance to the music of a jukebox. It was a large lake and was used for swimming and picnics. Mr. Dewey Rowan ran a used furniture store at one time in the Hamner building on Fourth Street. Mr. Ralph Condray had a radio shop on Fifth Avenue, the second door from the First Attalla Bank.

Mrs. Condray had a little hamburger shop in the front of the store. She made the best hamburgers for only ten cents. Mr. Condray always took his loud speakers around to all the all-day singings in the area in his panel truck. The Attalla Theater was located on the corner of Fourth Street and Fifth Avenue. Miss Myrtle Freeman was always at the window with a pleasant smile to take our dimes for the movie. It was an exciting night when Gone with the Wind first came to town. Roy Rogers and Gene Autry were the popular cowboy pictures on Saturday. Our Gang was a popular comedy, especially with the children.

Mr. James operated a ribbon mill that employed several people. It was located between Third and Fourth Streets, one block from Etowah County High School. Mrs. Holland ran a boarding house on Third Avenue. She later moved to Fifth Avenue where she ran the Holland Tea Room. The Bigham family owned a machine shop located at Five Points. The 1939 graduating class of Etowah County High School was the first class to graduate in the beautiful rock building which was built by WPA workers. The rock football stadium was also built at the same time. Stowers Hill was on the south end of our town and was named after a family by the same name. They owned a dairy that was sold later to the McClains. Later it was subdivided into lots. Many nice homes were built where the pasture-land was.

137

The Attalla Pipe Shop was located on Stowers Hill by the railroad. There were two service stations located on the hill. One was owned by the Clyde Burke family and the other one was owned by the Opie Reed family. Both men were affiliated with the Attalla Pipe Shop. Mrs. Casey Jones ran a florist shop on Stowers Hill. There was a large brick building on the corner where you turned to go over to the Pipe Shop. There was a café downstairs that was called Nick's Place with a hotel upstairs. Later the Bucklews occupied the building. Pauline Bucklew put in a dress shop, which was named Pauline's.

There were many hobos in those days. Many came on the trains that came through Attalla. They were often fed a meal on the back steps of the homes near the railroad tracks. A man was shot and killed at Nick's Place Café on Stowers' Hill. No one could identify him. He could have been a hobo. His body was carried to the funeral home in Attalla, which was located upstairs over some stores on Fifth Avenue. No one ever claimed his body.

Just beyond Stowers' Hill, you had to cross Big Wills Creek. When the big rains came, the creek would flood and water was everywhere. One time the water almost backed up to Stowers' Hill, but the houses nearby never flooded. There was a long wooden bridge with an iron frame top that rattled when you crossed it. Sometimes when it flooded it was almost impossible for cars and school buses to cross. The old Cherry Street Baptist Church was torn down and a beautiful brick building was built. The Ed Thornton's owned a grocery on the corner across the street from the church. The First Baptist Church of Attalla organized a mission on Stowers' Hill. Later it was named Stowers' Hill Baptist church. First Baptist organized a mission on north Fourth Street in 1950 and was named Northside Baptist church.

The Attalla grammar school was on First Street. Grades were first through eighth. The first four grades were separated from the others with a walkway between the two buildings, one wooden and one brick. The brick was a beautiful building with large white columns on the front with banisters on each side on the steps. Later a new grammar school was built on north Fourth Street. After the students finished grammar school, they went to Etowah County High School.

Some of the police that worked under Chiefs Glen Brown and Melton were Bill Amos, Troy Washburn, Ben Culvert, Ray Walker, and Ronnie Dickey. Mr. Swan, Ira Harris, who was called "Birdseye," and Cecil Folsom were motorcycle cops at one time. Cecil Folsom was a brother to the governor of Alabama, "Big Jim" Folsom. On the west side of town was a part of town called the Wilson Addition. There were coal mines there that reached all the way to Keener. Mrs. H. B. Copeland owned a large dry goods store on Fourth Street.

When Camp Sibert Army Base was built at Curtiston during World War II, they tore away the Pleasant Valley wooden church. Part of the membership built a brick building at Curtiston, and part of the membership went to Stowers Hill and built a building on Eighth Avenue. The lot was donated by John Coffee. The church was named Reed Memorial Baptist Church in memory of Mr. Frances Reed who was the Sunday School Superintendent at Pleasant Valley for many years.

Attalla was a booming town when Camp Sibert was being built and when the soldiers were shipped there. Some of the girls from Attalla married some of the soldiers. Many of our hometown men were called into service to serve their country. On Saturday nights the streets were crowded with soldiers and shoppers. It was a lively town. There was a commissary at the camp where soldiers and their families could buy items that could not be found elsewhere, such as sugar. During the war we had to have coupons also to buy gas. It was hard to find a place to live. Many had to go out of town to find a place. After the camp was closed, the area was made into a residential area called Siberton.

Memories of Attalla

- Margaret Yother

My father came to Attalla (I believe it to be around 1924). He took a job with B. C. O'Rear Furniture Co. I don't know how he came to choose Attalla. It was in the depression years and I think he must have known someone in Attalla. The O'Rear Furniture store at that time was on Fourth Street. They later located on Fifth Avenue.

Dad rented a house on First Street. Mother brought us children on the L. & N. train, and my first memory of Attalla is the depot. I was about four years old. The train stopped outside of Attalla at a water tank. (I think the train got water for the engine.)

There was a Heading Mill on first Street and an ice plant somewhere near there. A black man and woman lived at the far end of the street. They were very nice to us children. She had a beautiful yard with many shrubs and flowers. I don't think anyone thought it odd that blacks lived there.

I remember in High School years hardly anyone had a car. Several of my friends would meet at Walker's Drug store and walk to school. In very cold weather the boys would have bits of ice in their hair.

J. E. Smith had a grocery store close to where the post office is now. His daughter, Ethel, was a friend of mine. When we were in high school Ethel would sometimes work a few hours and I would go to the store with her. Many times people came in for cigarettes but could not buy a pack. They would buy five for a penny each. Bread was 5 cents a loaf. We went to Liberty Theatre movie for 10 cents.

A Condensed History of The First United Methodist Church Attalla, Alabama From 1851 to 1974

By Florence H. Little

In the year 1851 in a community called Newton, a group of Methodists met and discussed plans for building a church. It was located in the 800 block of North fifth Street. It was a crude log building with the cheapest of necessities. Twelve people organized and built the church. They had come to Newton with the first railroad and had been members of the Methodist denomination in their old homes.

During 1860 the Newton church bought a plot of land in the 100 block of North Fifth Street and erected a new church building. The old building was used for a short while by the Northern Methodists. They were few in number and soon disbanded and the property was sold to the Cumberland Presbyterians.

The new church was much like the old one, but it was of frame construction, the lumber having been hollowed from logs and there were shutters at the windows.

In 1870 Newton became Attalla because there was another town with the same name in Alabama and two post offices could not have been the same. Attalla was on the Gadsden Circuit and H. H. Cameron was appointed pastor.

The Attalla Circuit was created in 1874 and Theophilus Moody was named pastor. In 1877 A. M. Laurie was pastor. That year there were 45 pupils in the Sunday School and the church had a circulating library located in the church with 40 books. That was the first year there is any record of a parsonage. It was valued, as complete with lands and furnishings at $500.00. In 1878 there were 300 members of the church with 400 in Sunday School. The library was increased to 200 volumes, $16.40 was contributed to missions and $5.00 for relief of the poor.

In 1885 a plot of land was secured in the 100 block of East Fifth Avenue for the erection of a church. It was built and occupied that year. In June the Woman's Missionary Society was organized. A new parsonage was bought in 1887. It was valued at $1,000.00.

In 1888 Attalla became a station church with full time service by the pastor. The next year the church had 148 members and the Reverend J. W. Shoemaker was pastor. In 1890 the church was newly furnished throughout. New Pews replaced the puncheon seats which had been moved from the old church and a new pulpit was built. All this cost $939.90. This was paid in full during the year.

David Leith was pastor from 1891 to 1893. 1891 was the first year that any church records were kept, which we now have. For the time in 1896, Attalla was reported at the Annual Conference with its delegate, T. C. Banks. For several years Mr. Banks was conference delegate from the Attalla church.

J.O. Hanes came in 1900 as pastor. He was the first pastor to serve Attalla for four years. T. C. Banks was appointed to serve as delegate from the North Alabama Conference to the World Methodist Missionary Conference in New Orleans.

In 1901 the Woman's Missionary Society paid $9.00 on their pledge. By 1902 the church membership had grown so that another church was considered to accommodate the congregation. Mrs. Emelyn Bray (Robert) Forman gave the first $100.00 toward the new building in which we worship today. She began the drive for a new church because she was ashamed of the old wooden church on Fifth Avenue. Mrs. Mary E. Barnett McKenzie gave the quit claim deed for the lot at the corner of Fourth Street and Sixth Avenue.

At the First Quarterly Conference in 1903, a resolution was passed empowering the Board of Stewards to create a committee as needed for the building of a new church and to transact necessary business with reference to the building. A special session of the Quarterly Conference was held on February 3, 1903 for this purpose. The Trustees were empowered to borrow $4,000.00 from the General Board of Church Extension. The loan was made. The deed to the lot bears the date of February 23, 1903 from C. B. and Lalla Forman to J. W. Penn, Dr. J. H. Wood, T. C. Banks, P. L. Walker, Dr. J. H. Lester, R. W. Moffett, T. J. Bobbitt, R. W. Jackson, C. E. Stewart, Trustees. The deed was made for and in consideration of $5750.00. Not long afterward ground was broken with appropriate ceremonies. Mr. Edgar Lee said that any men members of the church were invited to come and plow a short distance on the lot, breaking ground. Many came. Construction began immediately. The basement was finished and used for some time before the sanctuary was built. Mr. Maurice Templin (father of May Cole, (Mrs. W. M. Cole) was the contractor. The cornerstone bears the date of 1903 –"M.E. Church South 1903." It is not definitely known if any artifacts were placed in the cornerstone when it was laid.

145

On Sunday, May 1, 1904 the congregation met for Sunday School and morning worship for the first time in the new church building (basement) - 153 were present.

$8,600 was spent on building the church. There were 44 members of the Woman's Missionary Society.

In November 1908 T. C. Banks was elected Treasurer of the North Alabama Conference.

In 1910 Attalla reported that it had no parsonage. In 1913 the Woman's Missionary Society organized a city mission and employed a worker for it.

J.D. Hunter came as pastor in 1915. He was the second pastor to serve four years.

The Fifth Street parsonage was purchased in 1916. The deed bearing the date of December 23, 1916, from C. E. and Melanie Stewart to Dr. J. H. Wood, T. C. Banks, Lamar Smith, H. B. Copeland, B. C. O'Rear, R. O. Noojin, E. G. Lee as trustee. It cost $2,621.58. R. O. Noojin was delegate to the Annual Conference in 1918. Three delegates represented Attalla in 1919. They were Noojin, Lamar Smith and T. C. Banks. D. C. McNutt was appointed pastor. Mrs. James R. Brown was president of the Woman's Missionary Society and Mrs. J. L. Botsford was corresponding secretary. In 1920 the Annual Conference was held in Gadsden with Bishop James Canon presiding. R. O. Noojin was again elected delegate. C. A. Tatum was appointed pastor. He was returned in 1921. R. O. Noojin and Lamar Smith were conference delegates. Mrs. Lamar Smith was president of the Woman's Missionary Society.

Lamar Smith became conference treasurer in 1922. Tatum was returned for another year. During that conference year on April 27, 1923, the Rev. Tatum died. His ministry had been great.

In 1925 R. O. Noojin became the second delegate from Attalla ever elected to the General Conference. A. C. Banks was the first. A. H. Nabors was appointed pastor. This was the best year financially. This year the pipe organ was installed. Mrs. Norma Bagget was organist until 1930 when Helen Easley Childers succeeded her and has been the organist since.

Mrs. D.A. Thompson was Woman's Society president in 1927, Mrs. E. J. Ray in 1928, with Mrs. James R. Brown as treasurer.

In 1929 John B. McFerrin Rice was pastor. Mrs. Gordon Isbell, Sr. Was president of the Woman's Missionary Society in 1930. The attendance at Sunday School was 280.

Mrs. C. R. Shepherd was delegate to the Annual Conference in 1931. Sunday School attendance reached an all time high of 335. This was one of the most difficult years financially.

In 1938 Mrs. J. Ralph Brown was conference delegate. This was the last year delegates were elected by the District Conference. During the year Mrs. Brown was elected District Secretary of the Gadsden District, a position she held until 1944.

C.C. Turner was appointed pastor in 1940. He was the first minister to serve five years. James E. Smith was delegate to the conference. He had the honor of being the first delegate elected under the administration of the united church.....The Methodist Church.

In 1945 H. G. Banks and Mrs. C. R. Shepherd were conference delegates. A. Tillman Sprouse was appointed pastor. Mrs. Helen Childers became choir director. That year plans were made for the erection of an educational building. F. Byron Todd was chairman of the Building Committee. Henry Culp, Sr. was chairman of the Board of Stewards and Mrs. Clarence Jones was president of the Woman's Missionary Society.

During 1947 J. H. Wood, Jr. Was chairman of the Building and Grounds Committee and led in the redecoration of the sanctuary and the outside of the church at a cost of $3,500. Henry Culp, Sr. was chairman of the Board of Stewards and J. Ralph Brown was chairman of the Building Committee. Some years before Gordon Isbell, Sr. had become church treasurer.

Mrs. W. H. Keener was conference delegate in 1948. Sprouse was re-appointed. He was the fourth minister to remain four years.

Ground breaking ceremonies for the educational building were held November 8, 1948. The cost of the building was $3,500.00 and the remodeling of the basement in the church was $5,000. $25,000 was borrowed from the Jefferson Standard Life Insurance Company. Gordon Isbell, Sr. was elected chairman of the Board of Stewards with P. L. Cameron, vice chairman, John Lyons, secretary, and Alex F. Farley, treasurer.

At the close of the morning service, November 14, at a church conference, the congregation voted to incorporate the church. The Board of Trustees for the corporation were E. G. Lee, chairman, R. S. Easley, Harry L. Hall, Gordon R. Isbell, Sr., Henry Culp, Sr., Frank Ledbetter, and Charles W. Burke. The official name of the church became The First Methodist Church of Attalla, Inc.

On Monday, March 21, 1949, the educational building was released to the congregation by the contractor and the following Sunday, March 27, the first Sunday School classes were held in the new building.

In 1952 the Board of Stewards was reorganized under the Official Board plan. Herschel Hamner was returned as pastor.

In 1953 Ford McDonald became pastor. C. B. McElroy was chairman of the Official Board with Melvin Freeman, vice chairman, C. R. Thompson, secretary…an office he held until 1964. George Hundley was elected chairman of the Board of Missions of the Gadsden District.

The educational building was dedicated by Bishop Bachman Hodge on Sunday, August 4, 1957.

The sanctuary of the church was remodeled in 1958. New light fixtures were installed. The organ was moved from the back of the choir loft to the front. Remodeling cost $28,845.58. A mimeograph and addressograph were purchased for the church office.

Albert Kaylor was appointed pastor for 1959-1960. Dr. Robert Pharr was Board Chairman, with T. J. Campbell, vice chairman and C. R. Thompson, secretary.

In 1960 Donald M. Mason was appointed pastor. The church roll was revised and brought up to date. In 1961 Linda Mathis was hired as youth director for the summer. Mason was a participant in the Preaching Mission in Panama. George Hundley was District Lay Leader. In 1962 Mason was returned as pastor. The L. E. Bradberry family was chosen as the Methodist family from the church and Gadsden District. The Lavinia Hunter Class remodeled their room as a church parlor.

Editor Martha Lou Riddle

Dr. John Sigmund Christian came as pastor in 1963. That year the old parsonage was torn down and the present one erected. The Parsonage Committee was composed of Gordon Isbell, Jr., chairman, John Lyon, Frank Ledbetter, George Hundley, Clarence F. Rhea, L. B. Todd, Dr. T. M. Owens, Mrs. C. R. Shepherd and Mrs. H. G. Banks.

In 1965 George Hundley and L. B. Todd were conference delegates. Two hundred hymnals were presented to the church by the children of Mr. and Mrs. Horace G. Banks. Mrs. W. D. Drake was president of the WSCS and Mrs. Allan Lee was president of the Wesleyan Service Guild. Jay Lowery became assistant treasurer. Russell Collins was chairman of the Official Board, Dewey Stansell, vice chairman, and Jack Haggard, secretary.

On Sunday, May 29, 1966 open house was held in the new parsonage.

In 1969-70 a new roof was put on the sanctuary. A new heating and cooling system was installed. L. B. Todd was Lay Leader. Clarence F. Rhea and E. E. McConnell, Jr. were conference delegates.

In 1969 Foster Talley served as Board Chairman. Mrs. Gordon Isbell, Jr. Was president of the WSCS and Mrs. C. R. Thompson was president of the Guild

In 1970 Dewey Stansell was chairman of the Administrative Board. Harold Walker was vice chairman and J. S. Roberson and Mrs. George J. Little served as secretaries. The same officers served the following year with the exception of secretary, Harold Keller. Johnny Norton was youth director for the summer.

January 3, 1971, Dr. John S. Christian died. After his death the Board decided to do without a pastor until conference.

Former ministers and conference staff filled the pulpit during these months.

William H. Bostick, Jr. Was appointed pastor in 1971. On Sunday afternoon, June 20th a reception was held for the new minister and his wife.

During the fall of 1971 a mother's Day Out Nursery service was begun at the church. Young mothers of the church and community left their children at the nursery each Friday morning for a day out.

Bostick was returned in 1972-73. Officers of the Administrative Board were E. E. McConnell, Jr., chairman, Ralph Culp, vice chairman, Mrs. Jean Dobbs, secretary, and Jay Lowery, treasurer. Charles O'Rear, Sr asked to be removed from the Board because of bad health. He was named an honorary member and so honored at the Board installation service.

In 1971 Bostick was returned for his third year as pastor. J. S. Roberson was Board chairman, Howard Malone, vice chairman, Mrs. E. E. McConnell, Jr. Secretary. Delegates to the conference were George Hundley, L. B. Todd, and Russell Collins. A teen room was formed from an old assembly room in the youth department and a significant increase in youth participation was noted. The week-day kindergarten expanded to two classes (4 and 5 year olds.) Teachers were Mrs. Lillian Clayton and Mrs. W. H. Bostick, Jr. Later in the year Mrs. Clayton resigned and was replaced by Mrs. Ray Lewis. The total enrollment was 29. During the year the Administrative Board appointed a committee to look into the possibilities of renovating the education building. In January 1973 Bishop Carl J. Sanders dedicated the parsonage after which open house was held by the parsonage family.

In 1974 Bostick was returned as pastor. Mr. Emory Boggs was hired as youth director for the summer months.

First United Methodist Church National Register

We who have participated in the writing of this book wish to conclude our remarks regarding Attalla on a happy note. The First United Methodist Church, which many of us belonged to, celebrated its 100th birthday on Sunday May 2, 2004.

There was a overflowing gathering of well-wishers and flowers and music and testimonies.

The catered luncheon was spectacular and the displays brought by long time members were sincerely appreciated. The showers of blessing were the tears of joy in the eyes of the members and guests

Now on the National Register of Historic Buildings we extend our good wishes for another 100 years to The First United Methodist Church in Attalla, Alabama. May you bend with the times and chart a mighty course.

FIRST UNITED METHODIST CHURCH - ATTALLA, ALABAMA

Printed in the United States
24482LVS00004B/118-177